Nearly Everything I Learned In Kindergarten Screwed Me Up!

by
STEVEN J. ANDERSON

Published in 2020 by The Yes Press

Copyright © 2020 All rights reserved.

Steven J. Anderson

Library of Congress Control Number: 2019916056

ISBN: 978-0-578-59247-3

First Printing Edition 2020

Printed by in the United States of America by The Yes Press, Dallas, Texas

The Yes Press • P.O. Box 92001 • Southlake, TX. 76092

Nearly Everything I Learned in Kindergarten Screwed Me Up! / Steven J. Anderson

Book Editor: Mike Steere

Cover Design: Jesse Brand

Book Design: Edward S. Brinton

CONTENTS

INTRODUCTION

BACK TO KINDERGARTEN, THEN BACK <u>FROM</u> IT

By The Author

For some time I've been cooking ideas for a book about lessons learned in early schooling that cause serious problems if we try to apply them as grownups. The book in my head, and now in your hands, would also provide age-appropriate, real-world lessons that need to be subbed in.

Some readers will recognize the title as a contrarian echo of Robert Fulghum's inspirational best-seller *All I Need To Know I Learned In Kindergarten*, which came out in the 1980s. Obviously Mr. Fulghum and I took different tacks. He celebrated simple little-kid wisdom that should be kept in mind forever, because it makes us better adults. I, on the other hand, focus on holdovers from childhood schooling that are hazardous to adult well-being and success. There's no contradiction, however. We're both right.

The line that became my book's title, about kindergarten screwing us up, was first spoken spontaneously to a large seminar audience. Unplanned, the words just burst out from long experience and frustration on the part of my clients and me. For years associates in my training and management company and I have dealt with people held back by learned helplessness and passivity and feelings of entitlement. I had come to recognize that this cluster of problematic attitudes and behavior dated to childhood. Grown people were thwarted by trying to be A-plus Good Little Schoolkids and expecting to be treated that way.

My core clientele have high-level professional degrees and credentials. They strive to make bigger things happen, but those who are grownup schoolkids fall short of expectations. Why? Because even at the height of their powers, at moments of supreme opportunity, they're like children who wait for some big person to say it's their turn. They wait to be called on, wait for the bell to ring.

They hold back, too, because they don't want to break rules they learned and took to heart long ago, which haven't applied for decades. They feel cheated of pats on the head, gold stars, A-plusses that nobody will give. Expecting A's for Effort is absolutely futile, because there's no such thing. Results, not what you did to get them, matter. But even epic results may not get approbation. If you need approval the way little kids need it, you may feel the need and suffer for it forever.

Many people struggle endlessly and needlessly because they're trying to live by lessons from a long-gone stage of life and follow rules that no longer apply. Some lessons of early life, if you don't leave them behind, make a mess out of grownups.

Ergo sum: *(Nearly) Everything I Learned in Kindergarten Screwed Me Up!*

THE REAL, ROOT PROBLEM

The problem was not and is not school. Nobody gets thrown under the big yellow bus here. Not teachers, administrators, counselors, specialists like the reading coach, or even the lunch lady. School people are heroes in our lives who deserve a thousand times more thanks than they get.

That was love and endless hard work, not abuse and stifling of the human spirit, when Teacher made us go down the hall quietly, two-by-two, raise our hands to be called upon, wait our turns and share, and on and on. We had to be socialized and taught to act in orderly fashion to be ready for years of learning to come. What we learned in kindergarten and subsequent schooling made perfect, absolutely necessary sense. Then one day it stopped making sense, because we were out in the great big world where we soon discovered that—

SCHOOL'S OUT!

Those who failed to notice set themselves up for trouble.

There's a word for the core problem here—**overextension**. This is a term of importance in child development, often connected to learning language. Little kids must cope with a growing gap between a complicated world and a lack of words for the things in it. They cover the gap by **semantic overextension**. If their first and only word for a quadruped is doggy, then a horse or elephant is a doggy. Likewise, a lion can be a kitty and all grown men daddy.

A lot of the most memorable, cutest things kids say, repeated ad nauseum to their everlasting embarrassment, are **overextended definitions**. Kids aren't trying to be cute, though. They're making strenuous intellectual efforts to extend what they know to the unknown. When they master new words, they dial back overextensions, and eventually only one kind of four-legged creature is a dog.

> People overextend all sorts of things, including lessons and rules learned in school at young, highly impressionable ages, when the world was smaller and much, much simpler. Those good lessons go bad when they're overextended into stages of life and situations where they were never meant to apply.

KINDERGARTEN AND PERSONAL CULTURE

In recent years I have come to understand and address realities of organizations and one's affiliations with others, both official and personal, under a very powerful and useful umbrella concept: **CULTURE**.

As defined in my previous book, *The Culture of Success: 10 Natural Laws for Creating the Place Where Everyone Wants to Work, Culture is a combination of beliefs, values, attitudes, and resulting behaviors in an organization...It manifests itself most in the group's behavior and communication habits.*

The words put the focus on organizational, group culture, as does the book itself. It emphasizes creating and maintaining a workplace Culture of Success top-down from a leadership position.

This book functions as a follow-up to The Culture of Success, but it deals with Culture at the individual level. This is **Personal Culture.** Changing a few words of the definition in the previous book yields this: ***Personal Culture** is a combination of beliefs, values, attitudes, and resulting behaviors in **You**....It manifests itself most in **your beliefs, thinking, behavior, and habits.***

Even if you never give a thought to Culture, as most people don't, it's inescapable, and it has a great deal to do with what you think about and do and the resulting outcomes, successful or not. Whether or not you're aware, as most people aren't, there's a dominant culture in every group with which you interact—working, at home, hanging around. But you bring another culture into the mix which is all your own.

If it's a good one, positive for you and those around you, you do it by design and by dint of effort.

A positive Culture of Success, organizational or personal, is almost never an accident. It happens because somebody makes it happen and keeps it happening. In the personal realm that would be you. Even when you're not on top, you can influence the ambient culture around you and manage your own by immersing yourself in the right subcultures. Even near-toxic workplaces and other cultures generally have good people to get next to. Meanwhile, you also manage what goes on in your own head and heart and live your Personal Culture in your actions and interactions with others.

Cultures are very sticky, and you don't want them stuck to you after you outgrow them. This, in essence, is the dilemma of grownups who are emotionally still in school and operating by school rules, which is the problem addressed throughout this book. Schools Out! is my shorthand for the solution. You've moved on so, you know, move on!

Serious stuff, but we'll have fun with it...

TRUE EDUCATION

And you will achieve results with the things we have fun with.

Don't expect a deep dive into the human psyche and inner healing. We hark back to ages five and six a lot, which resonates with developmental psychology and therapeutic systems, but this is really all about straightening out the Inner and Outer Grownup, not the Inner Child.

The overall purpose of this book is purely practical. I devote individual chapters to lessons from kindergarten and other schooling—each with the original version I call the School Rule and a new Lesson for Life to be substituted. I explain the Lesson for Life and how to apply it in the real world. You'll be given questions to answer and work to do to help get you moving in the right direction. Each chapter includes a **Results-Producing Thought and Action** section. Many include step-by-step mini instruction manuals for specific skill development. These are assignments for you to put in action the principles highlighted. This instruction is all in keeping with what I deeply believe is the best definition of education:

The only purpose of education is not knowledge; it's results-producing action.

More than just a definition, this is a complete philosophy of education.

Like everything my team and I do, this book is guaranteed. If you don't like it, don't get results from applying it, or are otherwise less than satisfied, just send it back with your receipt. If it doesn't work for you, it doesn't work.

On the other hand, if you like it and it helps you get more of what you want and less of what you don't want, tell a friend or share our weblinks and contact information. You'll get a hearty thanks from both friend and us.

So let's get started. Time to go back to kindergarten.

Suzie gets an 'A' for effort.

NOT NOW, SHE DOESN'T

If grownup Suzie still strives to get A's for Effort like the ones Teacher used to give her, she will be sorely disappointed. So will the organization she works for, if it even keeps her on the payroll. And I wouldn't count on that...

Just about everything we need to know about effort—and the expectation that we should be praised and rewarded for effort in and of itself—was uttered in two sentences in the original 1977 *Star Wars* movie. The speaker was the small, green, and all-wise being Yoda, Grand Master of the Jedi Order, who trained young Luke Skywalker to save the Galaxy.

Hero training was brutal. Luke bellyached about how hard he was trying, and Yoda said this:

"Do. Or do not. There is no try."

The space alien guru wasn't giving out A's for effort. Nor does the world. Real achievement that contributes to success, this is all a person can reasonably expect to be recognized and rewarded for.

What did Yoda demand from young Skywalker?

One-word answer: **RESULTS!**

That is the whole point of any effort worth making, however hard or easy.

It's also the point of this book, which is why this results-focused chapter comes first. If you don't get information you can put to work and achieve more/better/faster results that truly matter to you and your organization, the book does not justify your attention and time.

If you do get results, the effort you put into the actual reading and absorbing of the material is pretty much beside the point. Fine with me if you breeze right through it. Fine, too, if you stay up to all hours poring over every word. Feel free to memorize it, translate it into Middle English like Chaucer's *Canterbury Tales*, set it to music, prepare for brutal oral exams on it, and write learned commentaries that would earn A-pluses and academic accolades at Harvard and Johns Hopkins.

But it does not matter, not to me or anybody else, how you do it, for how long and how hard, so long as you find useful material and make good things happen.

At the end of the day it's all about the Do, not the Try.

Results!

HOW WE GOT TO BE 'TRY' PEOPLE, NOT 'DO' PEOPLE

As subsequent chapters will reiterate, we acquired what later became problematic attitudes and behavior at tender ages from well-meaning grownups. And they weren't necessarily problems at the time.

Teachers just loved to see our little eyes pointed down at books and papers or up on the board, a classroom full of kids hard at work, or pretending to be, as further evidenced by neat and complete homework turned in on time.

And there were lessons within lessons. Along with the actual subject matters, we were being taught to learn. This meant learning to apply ourselves and work at learning. We learned, too, that greater efforts bring greater achievements. It's true in academics, athletics, the arts, and any form of higher attainments that sustain us and enrich our lives throughout adulthood. Sustained effort to achieve and maintain mastery is a lifetime necessity.

On the downside, work for its own sake became a pseudo-result, irrespective of the fruits of the work. It survived in personal mindsets and workplace cultures that ruled grade-schoolish organizations. That's *ruled*, past tense, because grade-schoolish-ness exacted a terrible cost on complacent corporate America.

In the heyday of complacency, after World War II and before the disruptive shock brought by new, overseas competitors, workplaces were like great big kindergartens. Line employees in industry succeeded by showing up and staying busy, or at least looking busy. Same went at supervisory and management levels. At all levels the system rewarded activity, compliance, and shows of effort, whatever the results or lack thereof. The system worked, or seemed to work, for decades. But it doesn't work so well any more—not in today's workplace, no matter the industry or your particular job.

BLOOD, SWEAT, AND LOW-HANGING FRUIT

Sad to say, some leadership is still turned on by quarts of sweat—if not blood and tears— in workplace cultures that overemphasize effort for its own sake while paying too little attention to real-world results. Achievements are rated high or low by difficulty. Sweat cultists de-value good results that came easily, and pass up easy for the glory of hard.

Shades of school and A's for Effort, right? But the real world also hands out just as many A's for little or no effort. If success is just sitting there waiting for somebody to pick it up, the wise grab it, no hesitation or debate. As folks here in Texas say: Always go for the low-hanging fruit.

Some lifetime best plays are quick and easy dividends of opportunity. Never feel guilty about it. This is how the world works. You'll want to study your easy scores very, very carefully. If they're repeatable, figure a way to do them over and over and over, multiplying results. What comes easily and naturally may be the key to an overwhelming success system!

Remember, though, that easy victory is the exception. More often than not—way more—hard work wins the day. How hard the work has to be is dictated by the desired results. Achievers must be willing to do whatever it takes to get them. Necessary effort can be all over the board, depending on who's making the effort. But it doesn't matter if you have to do twice as much, or five times as much. All that matters, in the end, is your willingness to do the work, no matter what. And, of course, the results.

Back in school, a friend of mine gave me grief about the way I had to knock myself out to get high grades that came easier for her. Not only was this a friend who lived on the same block, she was a friendly competitor. Through elementary, middle school, and high school, we compared notes to see who got the better grades.

One day in a high school class, she glanced at my grade on our most recent math exam and exclaimed, *"Steve Anderson, you are not that smart. You just work harder than everyone else!"*

Guilty on both counts. I was not so smart, not in terms of raw aptitude. And I <u>did</u> work harder. All along, I had a realistic grasp of my innate intellectual gifts, which I judged to be pretty average. I reasoned that I had to make above-average efforts to get the grades I wanted. That's what it took, so that's what I did.

If you pulled up our old school records, you'd see that my high grades look just like my friend's. Who's smarter, who had to work harder to keep up, doesn't show. All you see are Results.

FAILURE OR SUCCESS?

In truth, there is neither failure nor success. We make subjective value judgements, labelling things and people as successes and failures, while in reality they're really value neutral. There are simply – RESULTS. Period.

Say, for instance, you set a goal to lose twenty pounds in the next ninety days. Then on the ninetieth day you step on the scale only to discover that not only have you not lost twenty pounds, you have GAINED twenty pounds.

So here's the question: Did you fail? Well, you got a very interesting RESULT! You intended to do one thing and achieved the exact opposite. You did not achieve your DESIRED result, but you did achieve a result. If someone else wanted that same result, to gain twenty pounds, you could tell them exactly how to do it!

Results: Desirable or undesirable. That's it. Fixating on failure or success clouds thinking and impedes progress toward achieving desired results. If the effort doesn't yield them, it's time to change the effort. You don't get the "A" for the effort. You get the "A" for desired results. So, beware the impulse to just redouble the effort and try harder. Doing more of the wrong thing might just get you twice as many undesirable results. You could gain forty pounds, not twenty!

ULTIMATE PURPOSE, ULTIMATE RESULTS

I owe a great deal to my first business partner, the late Walter B. Hailey, Jr., who imparted wisdom that I work and live by and share with clients. I will share some of it with you here and later, in other chapters. Walter was a revved-up, charismatic, extremely Texas Texan who built and sold a series of companies. Late in his career he started sharing his marketing and business communication systems through small, exclusive gatherings at his ranch in the Texas Hill Country. While I was in college, Walter and I struck up a relationship that eventually led to a business partnership in a training and consulting company. Though less than half the age of anybody else there, I will always be grateful to Walter and members of our early team for their generosity in giving my voice and efforts a place where we could all work together to achieve desirable results.

Walter boiled down the purpose of just about any
organization into a guiding principle by which all results
can be judged...

THE NATURAL LAW OF BUSINESS:
The purpose of a business is to create happy paying
customers, who repeat and refer and pay more than it
costs to serve them.

THE LAW APPLIED

The law applies to just about any organization that depends
on end-users saying *"Yes!"* and accepting what's being offered,
bringing in benefits greater than what it costs to get to *"Yes!"*
This sounds like profit, which is, indeed, an all-important
desirable result.

Money is not the whole point, though. There is a higher-level
result that is profit's bottom line: happy clients (by whatever
name you call them) who are so pleased with what you've got
that they keep coming back and bringing others with them.

Somebody says, *"Yes, I'm in, I'll take it!"* This is your pinnacle,
ultimate result. No matter how deeply you're buried at
headquarters, or if you code at home in your shorts and t-shirt
and you never meet a client and never want to, the efforts
you put forward must yield results that ultimately make it
easier for somebody outside the organization to say *"Yes!"*

and be sold on the organization itself. Results that don't lead there don't justify the effort.

SCHOOL RULES REWRITTEN

In truth, school rules no longer apply even in school—at least beyond the lower grades.

We hammer home the point to the youngest we work with, who are, in fact, still in school. Every summer through our non-profit education foundation, we gather an all-star volunteer faculty to lead a very special program for high school and college students. Eagle U is designed to give young people tools and skills to give them a seven-year jump start in their careers.

In each session I pose this question: What one characteristic or character trait is every college admissions department, scholarship committee, future employer, and future customer looking for?

The answers come pouring in:

- **Responsibility**

- **Honesty**

- **Reliability**

- **Hard work**

- **Creativity**

And so on. To be sure, these are all admirable and certainly desirable characteristics. But the ONE characteristic that everyone is looking for—and for which we all should strive—is the ability to get a predetermined, desirable end **RESULT**.

While hard work is important and usually leads to desirable results, in the end, it is the result that is measured most.

The point is reinforced by the top corporate placement firm, Cameron-Brooks, which has placed many thousands of junior military officers in corporate executive positions. Company co-founder Roger Cameron preached for decades a Gospel of Results: *"Don't just tell me what you participated in. Tell me what you accomplished—the real, observable difference your participation made. Show me how you made a difference in the end **result**."*

Top candidates who want offers from top universities and employers must show an ability to get things done which would not have been done without them. Being a hard worker with a great grade-point average and high achievement test scores are not the only marks of a winner. If that's all you have to show, it is not enough. It hasn't been for a long time.

What you most need to show are **RESULTS**.

In honor and memory of

Mary McInnes

My Kindergarten Teacher

She loved life, learning, and young people,
and instilled the same in me.

RESULTS-PRODUCING THOUGHT AND ACTION

ACTION A) THE YODA TEST

Remember to focus on clearly observable results that pass the test.

Restate what Yoda said—Do. Or do not—in question form:

Did I do it? Or didn't I do it?

To answer, you need to know what the *"it"* is, and it must be about what got done, not what you were trying to do, or how hard and long you went about it.

- **Yes, I did contact all eight board members and got five verbal commitments of support.**

- **No, I did not make a personal** *"Welcome to our practice"* **call to all new patients scheduled for tomorrow.**

- **Yes, I rechecked and emailed the quarterly sales projections.**

The above are acceptable answers. Yoda would be proud.

ACTION B) THE RESULTS LIST

Turn your *"To-do"* list into a prioritized Results List. Actions that contribute most to a desirable end result go on top.

Remember to focus on accomplishments, not effort. Then, at the end of the day, you can ask and answer, *"Did I do it? Or didn't I do it?"*

ACTION C) ETERNAL QUESTION

Keep a relentless focus on results and *"Did I or didn't I?"* Be results-minded in all that you undertake, working and living with conscious commitments to desired, intended outcomes, which you watch and evaluate real-time.

In light of results, ask yourself whether what you're doing is the best possible use of your time, effort, and resources. Be guided by the answer. When it's *"No,"* stop right where you are. Turn around, recalibrate, and go for the *"Yes."*

You didn't just try—you did it!

SCHOOL RULE

Do your homework. Work hard. Put in the effort. If you're working really hard at something really hard, you're doing the right thing. Praise and rewards will be yours.

- LESSON FOR LIFE -

Focus on results and what they're really worth, not how hard or easy it is to get them. Degree of difficulty counts in Olympic Diving and Gymnastics—not real-world success.

2

LET'S GET SERIOUS

STUCK IN FROWN TOWN

"Let's get serious."

"Wipe that smile off your face."

"Get down to business."

Remember these? We all do, unfortunately.

Over the years, I have been horrified to see my own offspring and tens of thousands of other young people being indoctrinated into *The Cult of the Righteous Frown*.

STARTING—WHERE ELSE?—IN SCHOOL.

I've always enjoyed the occasional lunch date with my kids at their **elementary** school. After elementary school, kids banish their parents from the lunchroom because that would not be cool!

A table or two is always reserved for students to dine with their parents. The children look forward to it, and it makes them feel special to sit in a separate, designated section. My first such visit years ago, however, almost convinced me never to go back.

As soon as all the kids had their meals and were seated, ten minutes of absolute silence was strictly enforced. The point was to *"get serious, get down to business, and eat."*

Who in the world takes a meal in unsmiling silence? Nobody, except maybe hardened criminals in solitary confinement. The *"serious silence"* took all the spontaneity and joy out of the experience. It destroyed the whole purpose for being there. Instead, my purpose changed to giving comfort to my child who was lunch-locked in an elementary school juvenile detention center.

Fast-forward to an afternoon recently when I lunched as a guest of our youngest at the same elementary school. Gratefully, the mandatory silence had been lifted, but not the punitive atmosphere. The faculty were still wardens and guards, the students still inmates. While we ate, a teacher patrolled the lunchroom to make sure all were behaving, raising her voice now and again to remind everybody who was in charge. Sensing my discomfort, my own young inmate pointed to the grownup on the prowl and said, *"Dad, that is why I HATE school!"*

I could not have said it better myself.

The Cult of the Righteous Frown still rules in the world at large, way beyond that lunch room. Many still believe there's something admirable about looking grim, that the faces of hard work, focus, purpose, and virtue do not wear smiles. If there's an item on the agenda—even just lunch for seven-year-olds—this is business you want to get <u>down</u> to, not <u>up</u> to.

Maybe America's Puritan heritage is to blame. The Pilgrims stepped off the Mayflower looking like lemon-suckers, and trying very hard to look that way, as if cheerfulness gets on the Almighty's nerves. Their Bible must have been different from mine, which heartily endorses the upbeat. Witness these verses from the Old Testament:

> *A merry heart makes a cheerful countenance, But by sorrow of the heart the spirit is broken.*

> Proverbs 15:13, NKJV

> *A merry heart does good, like medicine.*

> Proverbs 17:22, NKJV

Why do people in old photographs look so somber, like their best friends have all just died? Well, they thought that's how they were supposed to look, because happy faces would have made them look silly.

Thankfully portraits have changed, with *"Say Cheese!"* and *"Smile!"* being encouraged, but many in the work world have yet to catch up to the images. People still believe that to achieve serious results, and to be taken seriously, you must look serious.

Or, in two catastrophically wrong-headed, counterproductive, joy-killer words: Don't smile.

SMILE AND GET UP! TO BUSINESS

Describing a former boss, a close friend said that if the boss ever looked at you, it could be taken as a sign of approval or at least lack of disapproval, which were pretty much the same. If he ever looked at you and smiled, well, that would be a miracle, nothing less. This man never smiled, ever.

Not a fun place to work, my friend observed. The misery did not rest on the Sabbath Day, either. This boss, it turned out, was also the lay minister of a local church. Imagine the joy and uplift when he led worship!

No doubt this unsmiling character imagined that his stone face was right for work and righteous in the House of God, but he—and his face—could not have been more wrong. Not only does a *"happy countenance"* have the approval of the oldest management book in the world, The Bible, but it has the approval of modern behavioral science as well.

Over and over, experimental evidence has shown that people do better at whatever they're doing when they're cheerful. Smilers get more done, learn more, stay healthier, live longer, and recover from surgery more quickly. Science has also shown that putting on a cheerful face can actually make you cheerful.

Smiling, outwardly and inwardly, just works. People who are smiling and laughing learn more, retain more of what they learn, and tend to have a deeper commitment to using what they learn. You learn four times faster, get four times as much for your money, if you're having fun.

It's amazing, given all the evidence to the contrary, that so many organizations are ruled by ogres and trolls who imagine that high productivity looks like misery. The notion that work by definition cannot be fun or look that way is a disaster. Not only is the Unhappy Shop a spiritual blight, it's bad business. Smilers win over frowners in the market place, every time.

Money won't make you happy, but being happy can make you a whole lot of money!

Happiness is a magnet for wealth of all kinds. To him who hath, it shall be given.

GOOD CHEER IS NOT CLOWNING AROUND

Note, please, that we're talking about good cheer—not counterproductive giddiness or frivolity. An office clown performs for his or her own sake, to the detriment of business at hand. Chronic gigglers and laughing girls and boys are trying to dodge work. But the person of good cheer improves his or her own focus, and everybody else's, by shedding light.

SMILERS UNITE!

Like a lot of our lessons to be unlearned, this one got going in early childhood and was subsequently drummed-in throughout education, religion, and workplaces with anti-smile leadership.

We weren't born this way, not by a long shot. What happens when you smile at an infant? Absent serious discontent or discomfort, the baby often smiles back. Just a back-and-forth smile can have almost mystic power to bring a kid back from the brink of crankiness.

Smiling is contagious, as are the feelings that come with it. What's true of babies applies to grownups, as well, even victims of the Frown Cult. It takes a conscious effort to frown at someone who is smiling at you. Indeed, you can use the frown-back as a sort of litmus test. When somebody refuses to smile back at you, disengage, think of somewhere else you need to be...

Smiling taps into another major point of this book, which is that you create and sustain your own personal Culture of Success, which measurably affects the culture of groups you work with and live with. As the old song goes, *"When you're smilin', the whole world smiles with you."*

Start by smiling at yourself. Take a look in the mirror. If a Frowny Face looks back, brighten up. Do as a very wise high school English teacher once told me. Ms. Jane Scanlon was a very prim and ladylike Englishwoman, who was always using dry and veddy, veddy British witticisms.

One day I came charging into class and Ms. Scanlon stopped me cold.

"Mistah Anderson."

 "Yes?"

"Mistah Anderson, are you mmmm heppy?"

 "Well, yes ..." I said.

"Are you absolutely shooooa?"

 "Yes, I'm sure."

"Then kindly inform your face!"

UPSIDE MEETING OPENER

If you are leading a meeting, open with smiles all around, like this: Call on one or two people to recount, very succinctly, the very best thing that happened the day before or since the group last met. No fails, annoyances, disappointments, or problems, but only the win qualifies mention. Sometimes it's a reach, like something that made a catastrophic day a little less-so. But recounting the wins first thing in the meeting sets the tone of success for the rest of the time and potentially, the rest of the day.

Even if you are not in a leadership position, volunteering something that happened that was a success for the team can impact the culture. Speak up with an opener like, *"Would anyone mind if I quickly shared something pretty amazing that happened here yesterday, that you all should know about...?"*

Don't be surprised if somebody else jumps in with their own greatest thing that happened.

Never Forget—The Culture of Success is **You**. You can make a difference. You can always lead without being the leader.

HAPPY HABITS

1. Smile at everybody you see, all day long, starting with Yours Truly. Keep it up for at least 21 days, until looking like you're enjoying life is habit. If the results displease you, feel free to frown. (We bet you won't!)

2. Cease and desist from complaining out loud or to yourself. Avoid or tune out complainers.

3. Always hunt happiness at work and in all of life. Remember, what you look for is looking for you. If you hunt for things to anger, upset, distract, and disappoint you, you'll find them. But the seeker of happiness finds more things to smile about, over and over and over.

SCHOOL RULE

Work is something you get <u>down</u> to, not <u>up</u> to. It is not—nor is it meant to be—fun. Doers are dour. This is true in all important areas of human existence.

- LESSON FOR LIFE -

Smile and you'll have more to smile about in terms of measurable positive results at work, the rewards they bring, and colleagues who are happier to be working with you. You'll leave righteous frowners in the dust.

DO YOUR OWN WORK

DON'T BLAME TEACHER

Lest anybody get the wrong idea, I should re-emphasize that I am not impugning the educational system or good old Teacher.

What I'm really, really not doing is providing excuses and scapegoats. It's your fault and nobody else's if you are still, mentally speaking, sitting at an itty-bitty desk waiting for someone to write instructions on the board. Teacher wanted you to get up and leave when the final bell rang. Later your institution of higher learning made you put on a cap and gown and officially pushed you out into the world. Nobody at your college or professional school graduation said it in so many words, but the message was loud and clear...

School's out!

And school rules no longer apply.

Case in point: *"Do your own work."*

Unassisted effort often had a special value in school. At exam time, it was rigidly enforced. Teacher stalked the room. Just looking like you might be peeking at a peer's paper was as good as guilt. Giving other people your answers was as heinous as copying theirs.

There was a valid educational point: to provide assurance that answers reflected the current contents of our own, individual heads. Copying somebody else's work provided false and misleading data about command of the material and, ultimately, cheated the cheater of learning.

Made sense then, but it's a disaster now.

Why? Because **Copycats rule the world!**

THE UNIVERSE IS YOUR DATABASE

Nothing is more self-limiting than the holdover belief that copying others is cheating, that the only knowledge we're properly entitled to use lies between our own ears, that something accomplished in isolation is more worthwhile than a success patterned on somebody else's.

In truth, though, all of reality's exams are:

- Open book
- Open mouth
- Open ears
- Open air
- Open everything

Instead of grades, the world hands out riches, admiration, satisfaction, and happiness to its prize pupils. And those prize pupils—every last one of them—copy other people's work! They watch and study successes, thinking of ways to adapt what they observe.

Others' successes are your lessons in success if you're alert and clear-headed and use them as such. If somebody else has something worth copying, by all means do it, no hesitation or debate. Watch what he or she does. Eavesdrop. Listen and learn.

Imitating Mr. or Ms. Success may, indeed, be the most efficient method of absorbing what he or she knows, which you need to know. It is also the primal technique of education and self-improvement. Watching big people and imitating their movements, sounds, facial expressions, emotional responses, infants work their way out of the cradle and become walking, talking little people. Adults do the same thing. We can't help it. Whether we mean to or not, we're imitating people around us. So why not do it consciously, modeling ourselves on the best people available, for solid, self-improving reasons?

Kindergarten Heads, as well as losers of all stripes and persuasions, willfully deafen, blind, and handicap themselves by refusing to profit from others' examples and assistance. And they guard what little they know like the national gold reserves.

Some knowledge does, indeed, need to be kept close. The law, courtesy, and professional ethics recognize intellectual property and proprietary information. But such a rule denies us access to only a tiny bit of useful information. Beyond such exceptions, the world is, really and truly, an open book. Restrictions are mostly self-imposed.

One of your restrictions might be a gut-level aversion to the word *"copy."* If it makes you uncomfortable, try these:

- Emulate
- Duplicate
- Replicate

Successful people, in any field, by any measure of success, are those who know how to profit from the experience and knowledge of others. They watch what works and make it work for them.

THE C-WORD AND THE O-WORD

A little rearranging of what already exists is often all it takes to change the world.

That doesn't sound so creative, does it? Oh, but it is. Creativity is mostly the re-use of existing truths in new ways. Even the most startling and revolutionary creations of the human imagination are largely re-uses of earlier achievements. The genuinely new is most often only a small part of the whole, no more than a tenth, and usually not that much.

A lot of old with a bright bit of new brought us, in an eye-blink of cosmic time, the Temples of Angkor Wat, J.S. Bach, Count Basie, space exploration, the Internet, Texas barbecue, and all human-made wonders. If our ancestors hadn't been copycats—cribbing other people's answers—we wouldn't have any of it.

Here's another good, working definition of the C-Word:

Creativity is using somebody else's answers to solve different problems.

This is a good place to take a crack at the O-word: Originality. Just like Creativity, it's a great word that causes trouble if you make it an absolute value and a goal without understanding it.

"Original," according to Webster, means the first of the kind and something that is not a copy of something else. Fine, either way. The problems lie in the popular mind. To many people, *"originality"* sounds like a mark of value and excellence, like 24-carat gold and blue-white diamonds. People knock themselves out trying to be original, when they really ought to be concentrating on what works.

This insistence on originality can cut us off from the experience and wisdom of others. Just as bad, it can make us reluctant to exploit our own successes.

When something works once, originality addicts decline to do it again. They dream up something new and different and admire themselves for making the effort. But there's nothing to be admired here—we're looking at self-defeat!

When you examine it closely, nothing—invention, work of art, recipe, song—is really all that original.Pointing this out is pretty unoriginal, too. As Solomon says in the Book of Ecclesiastes 1:9 (NIV), *What has been done is what will be done; and there is nothing new under the sun.*

Strive for excellence, profitability, beauty, and what you do will be uniquely yours, original. It can't be anything but. Originality takes care of itself.

When something works, figure out a way to make it work again and again and again. The great commercial triumphs of our age are mega-scale, mass successes— mass production, mass distribution, mass marketing. Modern empire builders figure out ways to make something happen millions upon millions of times. Nothing, at this point, could be less original than a hamburger, but some day our descendants will be eating them on other planets, sharing the experience on the newest iteration of a brain-implanted smart phone. Like previous iterations, the phone will be, mostly, a compelling update on what went before. The makers, as ever, will make brilliant adaptation of extant technology look and feel brand new and sell another billion units.

RESULTS PRODUCING THOUGHT AND ACTION

ETERNAL QUESTION*

- Whenever you see something that works, always ask yourself, *"How can I make it work for me?"*

COPY KITTEN TO COPYCAT

- Think of somebody close-at-hand, in your field or something like it, who gets results you want: a co-

*Note: You're right, you already saw an Eternal Question two chapters ago. There will be more.

worker, a fellow professional, a friend, a recognized success in your field.

- Watch what your subject does, listen to what he/she says. Pay attention to details but get the big picture, too. Anything and everything in view and/or hearing is fair game.

Analyze what you observe. When something jumps out at you, ask yourself if this is a component of the person's success. Could this do you some good? If yes, how? Compare yourself, mercilessly.

Experiment. When something looks promising, put it into action and keep it up long enough to give it a thorough, fair trial. If it works, make it yours, no hesitation or second thoughts.

When you get the hang of this, you're a copy kitten. Now be the Copycat and roam farther and farther from your own field and circles of acquaintance.

(Note: Later on, we'll progress to asking others to share what they know. For the moment, though, concentrate on what can be learned by following others' examples.)

THOSE WHO WENT BEFORE

It's true, we stand on the shoulders of giants, some of whom preceded us by centuries and even millennia. But we can do a lot more than just stand. We can profit by their examples and still-living genius. The books and works by others tell the stories of what they did and how they did it. Their achievements and creations show the way, too. At art museums, you'll see aspiring painters copy masterworks down to the brush strokes. The goal is not to become a Rembrandt imitator but to learn through imitation of the master, as part of one's own creative journey.

BRAINWORK

Right about now all the envious, self-sabotaging, and just plain evil, little voices in your head (we all have them) ought to be raising an uproar, yelling all kinds of reasons why you shouldn't be doing what you're doing. *"This is a betrayal of your personal integrity and self-respect,"* it accuses, or *"The guy doing better is a sellout and a suck-up and you'd never want to be like that,"* and on and on.

- Tell the voices to shut up.
- Get out of your head and into the here-and-now, watching and learning from everything that goes on and everybody who's doing it!

SCHOOL RULE

Do your own work. If you didn't learn it yourself or come up with it all on your own, it isn't yours—you're cheating if you use it.

- LESSON FOR LIFE -

Emulate. Duplicate. Replicate. Why invent mediocrity when you can copy genius? If it'll do you some good, copy anybody's and everybody's work!

4

NO, YOU CAN'T HAVE MORE

HALF-PINT SCARCITY MENTALITY

All this thinking and writing about kindergarten is like time travel. Suddenly it's 10:30 in the morning and here comes good, old Mr. Johnson from the cafeteria bearing mini-cartons of milk, one for each kid.

How many? One apiece, no more, no less. The fixed ration never changes but today and every day Teacher has to repeat it because somebody wants another one, knowing full well that's not going to happen.

Why not? Well, **there's only so much to go around**.

Same when we had special-occasion treats like birthday cookies or cake. Only so much of that, too, so everybody got the same portion, no seconds.

Even when there was a little extra, one-per-kid made sense because seconds for anybody would have brought on loud clamoring and out-of-control grabbing.

There was another kind of **only so much**. Think about the shiny new firetruck in the play room. Kids would stampede to get to it first, right? Playing with it would be a major, much-envied triumph that few would willingly surrender.

Teacher couldn't cut and hand around pieces of the truck, so she sliced up playtime. Everybody who wanted got her or his turn with the truck. Enforced sharing, wherein two or three kids played together, cut down wait time and equitably increased enjoyment.

And it all made sense. Teacher was right to curb the acquisitiveness of five- and six-year-olds. Without firm adult supervision, the aggressive alphas would have eaten all the treats, taken all the best toys at playtime, and generally hogged whatever was in demand. The rest of us would have been picking up crumbs and fighting over the broken dump truck and one-legged, bald Barbie doll!

Even-handedness, so everybody in class got their fair share, was much more than practical. Teacher also reinforced a prime human virtue and lesson for life. When something is limited or scarce and others can benefit from it, sharing is a moral necessity. Sharing really is caring—for others and one's inner being and the Creator. Great religions teach that charity, another word for sharing, is a sacred obligation.

As ever, though, the good stuff came with baggage that can weigh down grownups who hang onto over-extended versions of old kiddy lessons. For many, **only so much** ossified into a two-ton stone around the neck.

Call it **Scarcity Mentality.**

This zero-sum paradigm of life is also known as the Pie Mentality because it involves slicing up limited resources. With only so much, my more equals your less and vice versa. With scarce resources that don't divide easily, like the red fire truck, my more might equal your big, fat zero, zilch, nothing. Too bad for you…

Except no, it's not too bad, because it's absolutely not how things are. Not here in the real world where people take responsibility and initiative and tap into abundance—to our own benefit and others' too. Our world is not limited and constrained like that little kindergarten room.

School is out! We need to embrace **Abundance Mentality**, aka **Universal Mentality**, because our universe is limitless and full of good things, which we can re-make and multiply.

ABUNDANCE IN AN APPLE

There's an old story about a wise mother who taught the lesson of Abundance to her child with an apple. *"You can count the seeds in this apple,"* she said. *"But you can never count the apples in the seed."*

She was telling her youngster that good things can multiply, wealth begets wealth, bounty creates its own bounty, and ideas generate more ideas.

This isn't just inspirational Mama talk. No, it's solid, dollars-and-cents wisdom. We all possess seeds of Abundance and the power to team up with others and create more of what we desire.

ABUNDANCE GROWS UP

Out here with the grownups, everybody who wants a red firetruck can get one. We have options our kid-selves couldn't even dream about. Nobody could turn kindergarten into a profit center where the kids could buy a red firetruck for everybody. Kids couldn't attract investors and open a red firetruck factory. Well, we can! When we want more cookies, we can bake a triple recipe or start an online cookie business. If we're sick of being picked last for games, we can quit the team and form our own. And our team can invent a game better than any other game where we can be better than anybody else and beat the world. This is the power of the creative. There is always more to be invented, created, and designed.

More good news: The world does not grade on the curve! To my mind, this is one of the greatest idiocies in higher-level education, which for no good reason makes A's into red fire trucks. Only the top ten percent gets the highest grade, no matter how good the group's overall performance. The result is unnecessary pain and resentment and a frantic overemphasis on competition rather than learning. Meanwhile, out here in the world, anybody and everybody who does amazing things can earn A-plus-plusses and reap the rewards.

A new business booms and begets a new industry that begets new wealth, which begets newer, allied industries and more wealth. Getting and giving, taking and sharing, are often almost indistinguishable. Profitability isn't so much a measure of the money you can get from buyers but of what they get from the product, service, or ideas you provide. The greater the perceived value of what you offer, the more you receive. Getting rich is mostly a matter of enriching others!

ABUNDANCE AT WORK

The Culture of Abundance **is** the Culture of Success. This is true at the collective level and individually. Scarcity is the culture of stagnation and failure.

Beware of *"Mine,"* one of Scarcity's favorite words. My space, my stuff, my job, which is what I was hired to do. If it's outside my designated area of responsibility, it is definitely not my job, and I won't even think about doing it. Thus speaks the Inner Kindergartner, trying to hang onto her dolly and crayons. If she isn't careful, somebody will come and take them.

This attitude cuts all sorts of ways. For one, it makes for an uncooperative team member. A bunch of such people does not represent a team so much as a pie with slices of individual turf that people fight to protect. If the major struggle is to hang onto what you've got so nobody else gets it, how can you reach for more, or cooperate in harmony and make more? Difficult, if not impossible. So it goes in a Culture of Scarcity.

Ideally, leadership will see the light and embrace Abundance. But, as always, you can create your own personal Culture of Success by working and living abundantly. Let go of the narrow, reductive *"It's my job"* mentality and look for ways to grow your position and accomplish more to move on to bigger and better things. Look for ways to help teammates do the same without being invasive or intrusive.

Where recognition is scarce, create more. If you're feeling that little twinge of jealousy when someone else gets recognition and you don't, step up and say, *"That's great!"* Do the same every time something good comes somebody's way. Say it to whomever shares the news and to the winner. Say it and mean it. While you revel in others' successes, remember to glow about your own, too. Brighten the glow by thinking about why your success is good for your teammates, company, industry, community, and family. Throw in the country and the world. Let others celebrate with you.

We should stop and consider the one thing that everybody feels is in short supply. We don't just feel it, we **know** it's finite and dwindling by the minute. Talking about the minutes themselves—Time. Rarely, going on never, does anybody say there's too much time and ask for more to fill it. Why? Because there's never enough time and always too much to do for the time you've got. People blame our Modern Technological Times, but it was ever thus.

Here's a case where there is **only so much**, really and truly. You can't make more—not a nanosecond more—than the time you've got. You can, however, make more **of** it by doing more with it. Prioritize, organize, always awake to the possibilities of each minute. Instead of being driven through the day, task to task, obligation to obligation, leverage what you do to create more of what you desire. Time really is scarce. Make it abundant.

SCHOOL RULE

There's only so much to go around. The only fair share is exactly the same as everybody else's. It's wrong to try to get more, and really wrong to get it.

- LESSON FOR LIFE -

Abundance rules the world. Your more means more for everybody. Unless you're actually stealing, you didn't take it from others so go create more...for everyone. There's more than enough to go around.

5

LET'S ALL BE FRIENDS

SHE'S BACK!

Fifteen years post-kindergarten I found myself in deep inner turmoil because suddenly Mrs. Mary McGinnis appeared in my head and repeated all those old Teacher messages for us kids about niceness and inclusion, not leaving anybody out, and not saying mean things OR pounding lumps on each other.

It all came down to this: **Let's all be friends.**

It didn't matter that she wasn't actually there. When Teacher spoke, the inner kindergartner listened, and I felt really bad.

Here's what happened: In college, I started a new chapter of the largest social fraternity in the U.S., which gave me a lead role in vetting and selecting members. This was my first managerial experience in recruiting and hiring, and I knew how much rode on in/out decisions. We were building a brand and its present and future reputation, which would stand on picks for founding members. The fraternity wasn't for everybody, and everybody wasn't for it, and if we didn't choose wisely and well, we would not survive.

I knew all that, but this thing seriously messed with my head. Why? Because I still deep-down believed I had to make room for everybody and play nice. With imaginary Teacher in my head, I was not *"Let's all be friends,"* like I was supposed to be. Mrs. McGinnis would be very disappointed.

Or would she? In real life, she would have said, *"Get a grip, Steve. You're now a young adult in a new leadership role. You have the responsibility to make hard choices that have nothing to do with being nice or not-nice and friendship."* Mrs. McGinnis, who had a very level head, would never want her old child-appropriate lessons overextended and misapplied. I graduated kindergarten a long time ago.

But then I had that bad kindergarten flashback, which I'm glad to say didn't last.

IT'S ALL ABOUT CULTURE

Earlier in this book, I touched on the importance of Culture, which follows on my preceding book *The Culture of Success—10 Natural Laws for Creating the Place Where Everyone Wants to Work*. Old and unwanted behaviors and habits of mind revealed in this book you are reading now date to a legacy group culture, Kindergarten Culture. In this book we're all about **Personal Culture**, created by yourself for your own success in every dimension of career and life. To recap the definition: ***Personal Culture is a combination of beliefs, values, attitudes, and resulting behaviors in You...It manifests itself most in your behavior, beliefs, thinking, and habits.***

This is a working definition, in that the whole point is to update and upgrade your own Personal Culture, wherever it needs work.

This may be the most culture-centric chapter. It's about the all-important choices you make about the people with whom you will associate and spend time. Here, we'll focus on important relationships at work, where cooperation and teamwork are key. Other relationships get attention in future chapters. Depending on your position in the organization, you can't always control the people with whom you work. You do, however, choose where you work. In choosing where you work, you choose the people who work there just as much as they choose you.

GETTING ALONG WITHOUT GOING ALONG

Back to *"Let's all be friends!"*

Beautiful thought, but a lifelong burden to those who overextend it and knock themselves out to be friends with any and everybody, even to their own detriment.

Teacher really should have said, *"Let's all be friend-LY!"*

This, I believe, is closer to her real meaning. It's also wonderful advice. Harmony is the seedbed of happiness and accomplishment in the workplace and all of life, and you can do a lot for harmony by being friendly except when dire circumstances force you to be otherwise. Throw around friendliness freely. Friendship, however, is another matter. Here you must be very, very discriminating.

In and around the workplace, where your productive results and rewards are on the line, managing relationships calls for discrimination. Research shows that an individual's success level almost inevitably matches that of their circles of acquaintance. It's in your power to jump-start your own success just by associating with successful people. Or you can mess up by palling around with mess-ups.

To sort-of-quote Aesop, you will be known by the company you keep. It goes deeper than that.

> You are the company you keep.
>
> **And you are always free to keep different company.**

It's all ip to you.

FLOCK WITH CARE

While it's not all that original, we refer to successful individuals as Eagles. Our summer program for high school and college-age students to jumpstart success is called Eagle U to emphasize the point that You (U) can choose to be an *"Eagle."* In contrast, the *"birds"* who are heading in the wrong direction, who do not contribute to their own or your success, are Turkeys.

On the one hand you've got powerful avians who command the sky. When they see something they want, eagles swoop down and get it. Even sitting in a tree, an eagle is a picture of Nature's magnificence.Then there are turkeys. We're talking about the domesticated variety that can't fly like eagles because flight has been bred out of them. Ditto dignity and brains. They'll pile up and suffocate by running from shadows. Their pens have roofs so they don't look up and drown in heavy rain! Besides cheap, low-fat meat, their major contributions to the world are senseless noise and droppings.

Human Turkeys aren't that bad, and their failings are more matters of choice. Most importantly, they're never hopeless like real turkeys. They can change. And Eagles, however magnificent, can't afford to be complacent. They can change, too, for the worse. Pay attention, because this is important: Eagle and Turkey are identities defined by behavior, not states of being. What people choose to think and do determines their birdhood. Each of us, every day, chooses which we are. A good part of the choosing is affiliation.

Everyone knows that...

"Birds of a feather flock together."

And we have to be reminded that...

"Flocking causes birds to be of the feather."

So keep in mind that you have to...

"Be careful who you flock with!"

RESULTS-PRODUCING THOUGHT AND ACTION

THE FIELD GUIDE TO HUMAN BIRD BEHAVIOR

Before flocking or flying away you must identify species-specific behavior. Here are key indicators.

EAGLES

This one's quick and easy. Know your Eagles by the way you feel about them and yourself in their presence. Admiration, inspiration, pride to be in their company are giveaways. Meanwhile you just feel better, do better, and want to do even better. You look up, not down, to see Eagles. And you're energized. Generally speaking, people either add to your positive productive energy or subtract. Eagles add and make you want to do the same for them. If you feel drained and dragged down, no way are you dealing with an Eagle.

Given that Eagles are the birds you want to be and be with, this brief information might seem inadequate but it will do. You feel and know when you've met an Eagle because...you know.

WORKPLACE TURKEYS

This list of easy-to-recognize Turkey behavior is far from comprehensive. That's because there are innumerable ways to talk and act (or not do anything) in a Turkey-like manner at and after work. Fly away from the following:

> **WARNING:** Before you point your finger at a Turkey, take a look at yourself. No mercy. You could be reading about you and your own Turkey tendencies. No defensive gobbling and denial; just get real and change. More about this later. Don't be surprised if you recognize a buddy. More about this later, too.

WEATHER BIRD Starting here, because it seems harmless to have an in-house commentator to point out how much too hot/cold/dry/wet today is and what's coming next as if everything in life depends on the weather. A few weather words, no problem, but this guy becomes a distraction and a time-waster, hallmarks of a bona fide Turkey. You will never hear from a weather bird, *"Wow, isn't today gorgeous?"*

MORNING NEWS Worse than the first. Daylong gobbling about the latest news, emphasis on the bad and shocking or the controversial in order to start an argument. Either way, who needs it?

STAMP COLLECTOR What we call those who save up causes for anger at others, seething until they explode. Everybody on the team gets a page in the PO'd album, with nothing said about a *casus belli* at the time. But when the page is full, look out, because every unaddressed anger, going back years, comes out. Like a sleeper cell terrorist in your midst.

DESK WARRIORS Never at peace because every situation, however trivial, is perceived as win-lose deadly combat. Will try to one-up and humiliate others at every turn.

ALAMO MENTALITY Every feeble position and undesirable outcome gets a last-ditch defense. Turkeys get teary-eyed watching mental reruns of themselves being massacred.

SICK AND TIRED Or tired and sick. Coming down with the flu, up all night, way too early to be here, as if start time is something new. Whatever it is, it's an excuse and downer all around.

CRISIS A DAY A walking, talking major disaster on a regular basis. Casualties are those who have to hear all about it.

EYE-ROLLING All-purpose and undeniable way to be nasty, show doubt and disrespect, and generally dump on somebody else and their ideas.

BACKSTABBER Smile to your face until you turn around, then plunge in the knife.

BLAMING OTHERS If it didn't go right, somebody else messed up. Nothing is ever a Turkey's fault or responsibility.

TRIED THAT BEFORE, WON'T WORK Past failure justifies current inaction. Working out reasons why nobody should bother to do this or that is some of the hardest work Turkeys ever do. They're never constructive, with an eye on avoiding pitfalls and getting some new thing up and running. The point is Why bother? Also raining on somebody else's parade.

PROBLEMS, PROBLEMS Present difficulties jazz Turkeys even more than future ones. If somebody comes to you with a problem and tells you about it nineteen different ways without so much as hinting at a solution, what kind of bird are you looking at?

YES, BUT... Two-word opener for contrarian whose sole purpose is to be contrary. A dead weight in meetings or any communication meant to get things done. Look out, too, for, *"Let me play the Devil's Advocate here..."*

MAJORING IN MINORS This one kills the big picture with over emphasis on minor, unimportant details.

OFFICE EINSTEIN Unappreciated genius working far below his or her intellectual capacities.

POOR ME Turkeys require victimhood. Belief that somebody's sticking it to me is the world's most comfortable and oft-used explanation for subpar effort and results.

STANDUP COMEDIAN Devastatingly funny impressions of the boss and earnest co-workers trying to do a good job are entertainment staples.

WHAT TO DO ABOUT ALL THESE TURKEYS

Sure, you can smile and wish one and all well, but pull back and limit exposure. Silly as they seem, Turkeys endanger your reputation, performance, and productivity. Say *"Thanks, but I'm busy,"* when you get an invitation to flock. When you hear Turkey-talk in the office, tune it out. When a Turkey corners you and starts unloading misery and irrelevance, try this technique: Look at your watch, slap your forehead, say, *"Excuse me, but I just thought of something,"* and hurry away.

What you thought of is that it's not healthy or productive to be close to this kind of Turkey behavior.

NO, YOU WON'T MISS THEM

Not for long, anyway. Every time I give an Eagle/Turkey presentation, I get questions from people worried about being lonely without the good old flock. That lasts exactly as long as it takes to get next to an Eagle.

WHAT IF YOU REALLY LIKE ONE OF THE TURKEYS?

Go one-on-one and have a low-key friendly intervention. Tell this person he or she is too smart and talented not to bear down and focus. Unruffle their feathers by adding something like, *"I'm going to make some changes and take a shot at bigger, better things. Why not you, too?"*

What's the worst thing that can happen? The best is you've got a friend and brand-new Eagle, and you both practice soaring.

THE INNER GOBBLER

Self-discovery is never entirely comfortable. If you find Turkey tendencies in yourself, declare late November. Bid the inner Turkey good-bye. Then celebrate Thanksgiving. Learn to inwardly yell *"No!"* or *"Cancel!"* every time you hear self-defeating gobbling in your own head or feel yourself drifting back to your old flock and their ways.

The *"No!"* technique, by the way, is approved by clinical psychologists, who call it *"Thought Stopping."* But stopping only gets you half-way there. Soar with Eagles, thinking and acting their way, and you'll never go back.

SCHOOL RULE

Do everything you can to be friends with everybody. The more it costs you, the more noble you are for bestowing friendship.

- LESSON FOR LIFE -

Be very selective about who your friends are. Friendship is a gift, which should be given very carefully. Try to get along with everybody, sure. But don't go along with anybody, unless you're going with people you like, respect, and admire, who are headed in the direction you want to go. Quit flocking and start flying!

6

My name is Miss Jones

ME U.

"Good morning, class! My name is Miss Jones."

Thus was sealed an escape-proof contract. Teacher was a done deal, and so was schooling in general in a system imposed upon us. High school and college involved more teachers and freedom to pick and choose subjects and classes, but the basic deal remained the same. You followed a path set by others.

No, I am not casting aspersions on formal education. Let me reiterate, we owe our schooling a lot.

But even more, we owe it to ourselves to educate ourselves now that school's out. Professional success and personal fulfillment depend on lifelong learning. Unlike school, though, you call the shots.

Think of yourself both as student and president of your own university. Call it **Me U**.

In our networked world, Me U. has access to vast resources of written and media material. But the great repository of the most vital information lies in the minds of other people. True education depends on the ability to find people who know what you need to know and are willing to share. As in actual school, the faculty is the backbone of Me U. You must set high standards and recruit with great care.

Me U.'s tenured full professors are your uppercase-M Mentors, special individuals who share experience and wisdom over months and years. Selectivity here is two-way as you, too, must be worthy. Indeed, the Mentor makes the decision whether or not to take on the role. More on this and mentorship in general in a bit...

Meanwhile, just like at Harvard or Texas Tech, you have your junior profs, instructors, and graduate assistants. These are more casual, sometimes very short-term, informational contacts with people who can help you by sharing some of what they know.

In long-term mentoring or ten-minute *"How can I learn to do it like you?"* tutoring, your principle of selection is the same: The people you seek have done what you're trying to do and done it well.

If you want to learn piano, make sure your teacher knows how to play and play well. This should be obvious, except the world teems with the uninformed dying to pass on misinformation and share their ignorance. At least ninety percent of the advice nobody asks for is useless. It's worse, actually, because of the risk that somebody will take it seriously. If the blatherers have never done what you aspire to do, they'll explain why nobody can. They might seem sort of convincing. After all, they convinced themselves...

Be wise and take unsought information and advice with a grain (if not a truckload) of salt. Sought-out information from a person of proven ability and experience: this is something else entirely. The grains here are of pure gold.

And, just like gold, your sources of specialized knowledge and wisdom are where you find them. Yours might run the nation's largest and most advanced used tire incinerator. Maybe she's in leadership at your own company or somebody in an allied field you meet at the local Chamber lunch. Could be, too, you decide to seek additional training and credentials in structured programs such as a part-time MBA course or night law school. Only you know where to go and whom to ask, because only you know what you need to know.

Maybe you're wondering, *"Why should people share valuable knowledge? It's obvious what's in it for me, but what's in it for them?"*

Funny you should ask. In the past two weeks I've been tapped for two fifteen-minute tutorials in one of my areas of expertise, both times with people never previously met. Based on those and many such experiences, I assure you they can be very rewarding. Just being asked feels like a compliment and it forces the mentor to rethink out loud what matters most personally and professionally. It's educational for both people when the ask and subsequent contact are done with planning and purpose.

ME U. COMMENCEMENT

One of the most important things to be learned in true self-education—which you might never learn in school—is what's right for you. No one can tell you what it is; it has to be discovered through asking and learning from your own experience and the experience of others.

Go out and learn whatever you need to know from whoever knows it.

School may be out...

But education is forever.

Here's how you get it...

RESULTS-PRODUCING THOUGHT AND ACTION

MENTORS—EVERTHING YOU DIDN'T KNOW ABOUT THEM... AND DIDN'T KNOW YOU DIDN'T KNOW

The word we shall not speak

The M-Word itself, **Mentor**. Never use it in the presence of a person you approach as a potential source of information and insight.

People can be vague and all over the place about the meaning of mentor and mentoring. The words seem serious and heavy, like there's some kind of formal commitment. Think about somebody you just met asking, *"Will you be my Mentor?"* Off-putting, right? Scary, even.

So don't.

IRRESISTIBLE ASK

"Can I ask you for some help?"

This is the truth of the matter, isn't it? And the request for help involves powerful psychology that makes it hard to say *"No."* Part of the human inheritance is an automatic impulse to render assistance when it's asked-for or needed. Most cannot resist the request for help.

There's even more going for *"Can I ask you for a little help?"* It confers power on the person you're asking, acknowledging that he or she has superior experience and understanding that can benefit you.

We're still a ways from actual contact, but it's good to know the type of request to which your successful approach leads. You will ask for some help.

FIND THE GAP

Have in mind a specific information gap and the kind of advice you seek to fill it. Ask yourself...

What do I lack in vital knowledge, experience, and skills that would fast-forward my progress?

For gaps on your strong side...

What can I learn from those already great at what I'm good at, to build on my strengths?

Either way, analyze and think through specific lines of inquiry that will lead to clear answers that you can act on. Remember, you're not fishing for wisdom or trying to absorb greatness by getting close to it.

YOUR SOURCE(S)

Who possesses what you seek? This encompasses three questions...

1. Whom do I know who knows? Of the people in my acquaintance, who has the right resources, knowledge, or wisdom in my targeted area?

2. Absent a direct contact of my own, whom do I know who knows somebody in the know? Who has connections with a person who could be of help?

3. Who do I know of, that I would like to learn from, even though I don't see any connections or avenues of approach right now?

Case 1) gives you an obvious straight shot. With 2) you finesse an introduction through a person you know, who knows your prospective knowledge source well enough to make an initial approach on your behalf.

NOBODY'S OUT OF REACH

Do not be discouraged in Case 3), where there seems to be no connection whatsoever between you and your prospective adviser. Make your desire to meet a goal. Write it down. Keep it in mind. When something goes up on your radar, possibilities will appear. Then there's happenstance and coincidence, which can seem much more than serendipitous. As my team and I teach, what you seek is seeking you. It works for people, but only if you really seek.

Meanwhile, work the heck out of your direct and one-step-away contacts. The more people in the know you get to know, the more you're positioned to meet!

BRAIN CHECK

Before you initiate contact, do a smarter version of a gut check. Is there really a compelling reason at this time to request a one-on-one contact with a person who possesses expert advice? Can you find answers on your own? Would it be better if you held off and did more research and/or tried out results-producing action, so you know more and have work in progress to bring into the discussion?

KNOW BEFORE YOU GO

For first-time contact with a person of importance, study like you've got a final exam. Go online and reach out to intermediary contacts. There may be no need to bring up what you learn, but it will show in-depth understanding and your own confidence. And it spares you the embarrassment of obvious ignorance.

WHAT THEY NEED TO KNOW

To make your ask an easy *"Yes!"* the person should know...

A. Who is this, asking for time and attention?

B. What is his/her purpose?

C. How much time will this take?

The last point makes *"Yes!"* easy indeed. You want fifteen minutes, no more.

READY TO TAKE NOTES

Show up with pen and pad, prepared to take notes longhand. Yes, this is retro, but it makes a statement about your focus and attention that using a laptop, tablet, or phone definitely does not. Nobody knows for sure what people are doing onscreen. You can't secretly message friends or shop on paper.

LISTENING AND LEARNING

So here you are in direct contact, listening and learning face to face or in a call. Congratulations! Seriously. You have taken a mature step toward success and personal enrichment.

Right now you are a student. A good one pursuing independent studies. You arrive prepared with intelligent, thought-through lines of inquiry. You seek to start building a knowledge base and skill set like that which your Mentor possesses.

You want understanding, not just simple answers. You are absolutely not asking somebody to solve problems for you. It's fine to bring up current challenges, but your goal is to learn how to handle them yourself with the help of your Mentor's expert input and advice.

TIME'S UP

Call time when the promised fifteen minutes is up. Respectfully, of course. If the Mentor wants to keep talking, fine, but that will be his or her clear preference and decision. Even then, watch for signs of flagging interest or fatigue. Remember the old showbiz saying—Always leave them wanting more.

NEXT TIME

Open the door for follow-up by asking for permission to check in, to let them know about what you accomplish with what you just learned. From the Mentor's point of view, this is engaging and flattering.

MENTORSHIP UPGRADE

The relationship may well deepen if the person likes you and appreciates your mind and use of what you learn. When it happens, it's extremely rewarding on both sides and potentially life-changing for you. But the decision to upgrade to capital-M Mentor, a role exalted through the ages, is up to her or him and not you. Your part is to do all you can with what you learn, tell about it, and express heartfelt gratitude and appreciation.

INFORMATION FROM WORKPLACE PEERS

Paradoxically, it can seem easier and lower-risk to seek mentoring from higher-ups in prestige and power, than from somebody you see all the time who's at your same level in your organization. The object may be to get as good as others, but never straight-out ask them to tell or show how they do it. Instead, appeal to their greater experience and expertise, which you admire—you do, or you wouldn't be picking their brains—and ask how you can learn to get so good, too.

MENTOR-SURFING & STRAIGHT TALK FROM UNCLE HOWARD

Some of my earliest and most meaningful Mentor experiences came during my last year of college when I went Mentor surfing coast to coast. I had highly informative and inspirational conversations with more than sixty of the country's most powerful business leaders. That adventure in learning from the experts made all the difference in my life.

My quest for understanding was more personal than the clear, results-oriented lines of inquiry I recommend in this chapter. Bear in mind that I was still in school, though the nervous thrill of *"School's Out!"* was coming up fast and I had decisions to make about my career path and ultimate aspirations. I wanted to ask supremely accomplished individuals how they had found their own directions and made decisions that got them to their pinnacles of success.

I initially turned to my closest relationships who had a vested interest in my success. One was my dad's brother Howard Anderson. A major success in the broadcasting business, he had connections with no end of shakers and movers and generously opened his entire network to me. Not only did he ask big-deal friends to sit down with me, he set up many of the meetings.

Uncle Howard also gave me some straight talk I'll never forget: *"I want you to understand that I'm introducing you to a life's work of important relationships."* He fixed me with a stare and said, *"Don't screw it up!"*

Thus he drove home a critically important point. When people connect you to others important to them, they're not doing you a small favor. They're doing you a big favor and putting a great deal of trust in you, because the impression you make reflects back on them. We call this **borrowing influence.** As my Uncle Howard memorably advised, *"Don't screw it up!"*

Of the many people Uncle Howard introduced me to, one was a top executive who had held positions in three U.S. presidential administrations and had run several publicly traded companies. Up front, I promised that I would only take fifteen minutes of his valuable time. After fifteen minutes, he insisted that I stay. That conversation lasted more than two hours! Why? Because we were talking about the most important person in his life. Himself. How often does that happen for most people? He did all the talking and I did all the asking. His feedback to my uncle was that I was the most intelligent young man he had ever met, which was a totally subjective opinion. There was no way he could have measured my intelligence. All he knew was that he felt better because of our meeting together. I gained from his valuable experience. He reflected on and revisited the most important aspects of his success. And the relationships between all involved were left improved. Mission accomplished!

Focused on those who had done what I aspired to do—build an organization from the ground up—I picked up very clear ideas about many components of success and excellence. On the other hand, I saw business after business I didn't want to get into. Much as I was enriched and inspired by the time with many different Mentors, I walked away knowing as much about what I did not want to do as I did about what I wanted to do.

The journey helped educate my intuition, for I was picking up bits and pieces about myself from the experience of others, so that when the right opportunity presented itself, I knew it was the one for me.

SCHOOL RULE

Teacher is picked for you not by you, in a system not of your making. What you learn, when, and how you learn it is up to others.

- LESSON FOR LIFE -

School for grownups is the whole world, for all of life. Education is yours to be had from anybody anywhere who knows what you need to know. The only option you don't have is to quit learning.

7

Any Questions?

ASK-A-PHOBIA

The first day of my high school Calculus class was mostly nuts and bolts about material to be covered, the teacher's expectations and grading system, and other need-to-knows for maximum learning and good grades.

Somewhere in the mix, a good buddy of mine raised his hand and asked a question. What it was, I cannot recall, except that it seemed reasonable and fair game. Had my friend gotten an answer, this incident would be lost and long forgotten.

But the teacher planted both hands on his desk, leaned forward, looked down from a great Olympian height and sneered at my friend and all mortals silly enough to ask such a question. Nobody can do public shaming like a secondary school educator who's had years of practice. This guy obviously enjoyed it, too.

He said...

Wait for it...

"Duh."

There it was, the lesson of the day and one of my most vivid memories of Calculus class. Unpack the "Duh," and you get, *"Unless you want to look like an idiot in front of the whole world, **don't ask any questions."***

Sad—no, tragic—to say, this was more like a Lesson for Life that's baked into our experience growing up. By the time we master long division, we've all been stung by the likes of Mr. Contemptuous in Calc. With questions left unanswered, they asked why on Earth we were asking. That material has already been covered, hasn't it? Asking meant we were worse than ignorant. We were lazy, daydreaming in class, skipping homework. If you paid attention and did your work, you wouldn't need to ask, would you?

We are the end-products of a system that stifles the natural eagerness to make inquiries out loud and in person—to ask. Every year, from kindergarten on, each interrogative sentence feels a little bit more hazardous than the one before it. Asking seems less and less like a way to satisfy curiosity and gain needed information, and more like a chance to embarrass oneself and lose face.

We were not born question-phobic, not by a long shot. As soon as we could make intelligible sounds, we were asking.

"Why, Mom?"

"How come, Dad?"

"What for, Grandma?"

Kids are question machines, to an extent that can drive you crazy.

But the endlessly curious child, wanting to know why planes can fly but SUVs can't, why Kitty can't bark, isn't a tenth as maddening as the risk-aversive mutes graduating from universities, who are far more afraid of looking dumb than being dumb and try like crazy never to ask anybody about anything.

Average five-year-olds ask more than 50 questions a day. Average adults with advanced degrees and professional credentials are reluctant to ask more than two, and one of those is usually something really intelligent like, *"Where's the bathroom?"* There's half their question quota for the day!

Among the major missions of my career is helping people battle ask-a-phobia, which is rampant among pretty much everybody beyond the second grade.

In just about every seminar we present around the world, the room has a sign that reads in big, bold letters:

QUESTIONS ARE THE ANSWER

Asking makes you smarter in every single way you can be smart:

- In knowledge
- Effectiveness
- Productivity
- Deal-making business savvy
- Emotional understanding
- Likability
- Even lovability

What keeps people from asking, and getting smarter? The fear of rejection and looking dumb.

Think about the last time a person in a leadership position or position of authority said, *"Any questions?"* There was the uncomfortable silence. All present looked blank and felt squeamish. If a lively give-and-take ensued, count yourself very fortunate. Much of the time, *"Any questions?"* doesn't sound or feel a bit like an invitation for clarity and further understanding. It's more like a great big *"Duh!"*

The thing to fear is not *"Duh!"* but the price to be paid for not asking for what you need to know. Ask the right people the right ways at the right moments and you'll never want to stop. You won't stop asking, either. And you'll wonder why it ever seemed scary.

GIVE MY OLD PROFESSOR A MEDAL

Primary and secondary education, however, are nothing compared to the college experience. When Dr. Vicious, PhD and SOB, asked, *"Any questions?"* only the most iron-clad egos and the foolhardy raised their hands. Whatever questions they had, they'd whisper to each other, or not ask anybody.

But then, one day, a professor of mine amazed me and everybody else by breaking precedent.

I should explain that *"ask aversion training"* had little or no effect on me. I was and still am a committed, enthusiastic, all-occasion asker. Every session I peppered this particular prof with questions, until one day the man stopped and pinned me to my seat with a particularly terrifying scowl.

"Anderson, do you always ask so many questions?"

Thinking *"Uh-Oh,"* I answered somewhat tentatively, *"Well, yes I do."* The class was holding its breath.

"Don't stop," he said. *"Now let that be a lesson to the rest of you,"* as he turned talking to the rest of the class. *"If you haven't noticed, Mr. Anderson has single-handedly controlled the curriculum of this class so far this semester just by virtue of the questions he has been relentlessly asking. That stops today, Mr. Anderson, because I have to get this class back on track!"*

While he let me know I should back off and not try to take over the class anymore, he did tell me and everybody else to ask and keep asking. He or she who speaks up and asks questions has the power to profoundly influence the flow of information vital to understanding and success. For this he truly does deserve a medal. Such largeness of intellect and spirit is, unfortunately, rare.

Thinking *"Uh-Oh,"* I answered somewhat tentatively, *"Well, yes I do."* The class was holding its breath.

"Don't stop," he said. *"Now let that be a lesson to the rest of you,"* as he turned talking to the rest of the class. *"If you haven't noticed, Mr. Anderson has single-handedly controlled the curriculum of this class so far this semester just by virtue of the questions he has been relentlessly*

asking. That stops today, Mr. Anderson, because I have to get this class back on track!"

While he let me know I should back off and not try to take over the class anymore, he did tell me and everybody else to ask and keep asking. He or she who speaks up and asks questions has the power to profoundly influence the flow of information vital to understanding and success. For this he truly does deserve a medal. Such largeness of intellect and spirit is, unfortunately, rare.

RESULTS-PRODUCING THOUGHT AND ACTION

ASKERS ALMANAC

DUMB QUESTIONS

The old saying goes that there's no such thing as a dumb question. Wrong! There are millions of dumb questions.

All are alike in at least one respect—they insult the intelligence of somebody, if not everybody.

Never, ever –

Ask anybody up the leadership ladder or down: *"How do I do my job?"*

Ask when it's easy to figure out or research the answer yourself: *"Which way is up?"*

Ask a high-level expert low-level questions: *"Dr. Eminent Scientist, does gravity make stuff fall? What's three percent of 200?"*

Ask just to fish for information, without a good, thought-through idea of what you want to know and confidence that the person you're asking knows.

Ask to deliberately expose another person's ignorance, or otherwise humiliate or hurt.

Ask just to be noticed.

GOOD QUESTION!

Forethought and purpose make all the difference. Begin by questioning yourself: You may know more than you think you know, so you don't need to ask. If you're feeling a knowledge gap, think it through so you know exactly where it lies and what it will take to fill it. Know why this missing information is important to you and why you need it now. Be sure, too, that the person you're asking is very likely to possess it.

It's very important to frame and direct your questions carefully so the answers bring you the information you need. Separate the issues, and speak to the issues.

The Smart Question is, in every respect, the polar opposite of its Dumb counterpart. It flatters and empowers everybody involved—you, the person you're asking, the people listening-in. The information elicited will do some good, and the exchange of information feels good. Indeed, a fruitful Q&A is one of the most thrilling and satisfying forms of human contact.

ASKING UP

We're talking about high-ups on the leadership ladder with power to affect your professional and personal destiny. Because there's more at stake, it's important to do your pre-asking work with special care. But don't be timid. With good groundwork, the very act of asking can show that you're performing the critical on-the-job task of the Information Age: you're gathering data, thinking about it, and using it to solve problems.

If a specific problem prompts your asking, aim your question(s) straight at it.

Before you ask, come up with a couple thought-through, plausible solutions. Unless circumstances absolutely force you to do it, don't ask empty-handed.

THE PROTOCOL FOR ASKING UP

Frame your inquiry and say why it's important and timely:
"Charlene, there is a situation that needs to be addressed..."

Tell, briefly but clearly, about the solutions you've already come up with: *"Would it make sense if we...?"*

Appeal to the person's greater experience and expertise, and ask for input: *"I'm sure you have dealt with similar situations. Is that what you would recommend?"*

Maybe one of your proposals will be embraced as-is or with modifications. But even if he or she has a better idea, you enhance your position by coming with ideas. Nobody will think you're asking the Career-Killer Dumb Question: *"What should I do?"*

Once you've got the information, ask if you can keep the other person informed about progress. Do so, without overdoing it, and you'll tap into a continuous flow of freely-given information to help your performance.

There's an ultimate question behind all queries to a person in leadership:

"What is the most important RESULT that I can help bring about?"

Now and again, especially in more general talk and periodic performance reviews, the question can seem perfectly natural. It's amazing, considering how vital to success the answer is, how seldom people think to come out and ask.

Ask-up principles apply with clients and customers, too. You need to ask what's most important to them about whatever your organization provides. The better you understand them and their needs, the better you can meet those needs. And the more business they'll do with you, while referring others.

ASKING DOWN

For the insecure in a position of authority, this can be more uncomfortable than asking up. The idea seems to be that the one in charge should know absolutely everything, so asking makes you less of a leader. This is dead wrong. Real leadership is bolstered by soliciting information, opinions, and viewpoints from everybody. Team members work harder, and better, because somebody respects what they know and believe. The more the leader asks, the more the leader knows, and the more effective the leader can be. Being effective, not bossy, is where real authority lies.

Besides making you smarter, asking for information and input is an enormous morale-booster. Asking takes care of the number-one complaint in management-employee relationships: that nobody in authority listens.

Always ask with respect and attention, giving others power to answer confidently and freely. With longstanding team members, appeal to their experience and accumulated knowledge: *"Bill, I need your help. I'd like to pick your brain for a minute..."*

LATERAL ASK

Seems like this one ought to be easiest, right? After all, where's the risk with somebody at your own level? But there's a lot to discourage frank exchanges, like territoriality and protectiveness about one's own position and general silo mentality about jobs, even amongst people who sit next to each other with shared responsibilities. Break down the barriers by showing sincere interest in how things work and look from your peer's point of view. Ask what changes you could make that would be helpful. Don't be surprised if you get the same question.

WASTE NOT, WANT NOT

Nobody has time for a Time Waster! Be quick and to-the-point without being abrupt. Treat everybody you ask as if they're billing you the highest hourly rate from the second you open your mouth. In today's overbooked world, time has as much or more value than money. Honor others by doing your pre-ask groundwork so you know what you need to know, and how you're going to ask.

TAKE THE PLEDGE

I, _____ *(your name)*, do
solemnly swear to fill all my information gaps in all areas
of life every single day by asking people qualified to answer
GOOD QUESTIONS.

I pledge to USE what I learn as soon I learn it, and to go on
asking and learning in perpetuity.

_____

(Date)

_____

(Signature)

_____

(Witness Signature)

SCHOOL RULE

Don't ask. Even if the question is smart, it will probably make you look dumb. Asking is public admission of ignorance, inviting all sorts of risk.

- LESSON FOR LIFE -

Ask, ask, and ask some more. Asking is the *"Open Sesame!"* to all of the world's riches. Asking the smartest people smart questions is the best way to get smart and show the world just how smart you are.

DON'T INTERRUPT

THE GREAT WALL OF BLAH BLAH BLAH

H uman beings are born interrupters. When babies have something to share, they open their mouths and let it rip. It's too bad if everybody's asleep or Mommy and Daddy are working on their joint Nobel Prize acceptance speeches.

Before long Baby goes from squalling to cute noises then words and sentences and more and more interesting reasons to want to be heard. But adults stifle kids with, "Don't interrupt," or the retro throwback, "Speak only when spoken to," or at school, "Wait until you're called on." And the poor kids are on the road to a lifelong reluctance to break in and speak one's piece or ask a question.

When somebody, particularly somebody important, talks with others or seems preoccupied, the average adult wanting to go over and say something suffers abject tongue-tied paralysis. When he or she does work up the nerve, dignity and credibility don't stand a chance. A person who interrupts with 1,500 inner voices screaming "Don't!" is not pretty to behold.

Interruption phobia is worse than a vow of silence, because you're mute exactly when speaking will do the most good! If you don't get good at interrupting, you may never get to meet the people you deserve to meet or see your fondest wishes realized. You will stand forever on the wrong side of the Great Wall of Blah Blah Blah and be trapped at the foot of the I'm-Doing-Something-Important Mountains. Everybody is always talking and always busy.

MITIGATING RISK

As are all aspects of interpersonal communication, interruption is a learned skill that you can work on and practice until it feels natural and even enjoyable. With an artful interrupter, people barely notice they've been interrupted and then totally forget as their attention shifts to the valuable contribution that the newcomer makes to the conversation.

Of course, this isn't going to happen if you don't put something delicious on the conversational table. And, no matter how brilliant your contribution, it won't happen if you obnoxiously barge in.

Never forget that there's an excellent reason why interrupting feels risky. It is risky! Shove your way into somebody else's conversation when you don't belong in it, jump in with comments at a meeting when you have no real contribution to make, and you have announced to all present that you are a fool.

As the old joke goes: Why just stand there like an idiot, when you can open your mouth and remove all doubt?

That's exactly what artless interrupters do.

RESULTS-PRODUCING THOUGHT AND ACTION

THE ARTFUL INTERRUPTER

THE BASICS

Key interruption challenges fall into two categories

A. THE VIP Here your goal is to make a connection with the person who is a Big Deal, that you haven't met, who's in conversation with others. The usual setting is a social period at a business-related event: after-speech reception, cocktail hour, mealtimes, or between-session breaks.

B. THE MEETING This can be any sort of discussion conducted somewhat informally, i.e. without the benefit of Rules of Order and a chairman—the role taken by Teacher back in school—to recognize speakers. Your goal is to break into the flow and grant yourself the privilege of speaking.

Certain fundamental principles apply to both.

- If there isn't something solid to be gained, forget it. What's in it for you is less important than what's in it for those you've interrupted. Be sure your words are timely and pertinent.

- Relying on charm and wit to excuse you is a mistake. Ditto good looks.

- Begin by getting in sync. Watch and listen, so your expression and mood mirror that of your target person or group.

- When you make your move, "Excuse me" or maybe "Excuse me for a second" is all it takes.

- Do not open with an apology, because that says you have something to apologize for. Never use the word "interrupt" when you're interrupting! "Sorry to interrupt," is a double fail.

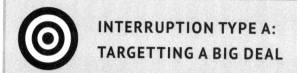

INTERRUPTION TYPE A:
TARGETTING A BIG DEAL

PREPARATION

The more you find out and do up front, the better the outcome.

If you possibly can, pre-engineer an introduction or at least prior knowledge of who you are, so you don't do a stone-cold interruption of an important individual, which might be awkward and irritating.

Ideally you can go in under the wing of another personage known to your target. Let's say you're going to an awards event and have a good reason to want to talk with a famous author giving the keynote.

Check around to determine who you know who's going to be there. Maybe you're on good terms with a pretty big deal who will be there who knows your target. If so, say something like, "Mike, I would really like to meet Ms. Famous. Would you be willing to introduce me to her, since you already know her?"

Even if Mike doesn't ask, say why you want the introduction. Maybe you'd like to interview Ms. Famous for your podcast. Whatever it is, it has to be more substantive and of interest to the target than just, *"Oooh, I want to meet because I am such a big fan. And I want an autograph and a selfie!"*

Be mindful that you're asking for a real favor from Mike, who puts his standing and influence on the line. *Borrowing influence* is one of the most effective strategies to establish contact and gain respectful attention you would not get all on your own. But it's also like borrowing a car in that influence is worth a lot and you want to be very, very careful to return it spotless with the gas tank replenished. Be appropriately appreciative, too.

Even if Mike won't be at the event, you can ask if he's willing to email or otherwise reach out so your target expects you to introduce yourself at the event. Ask Mike to say something to the effect that **he suggested to you that you come up and introduce yourself for such-and-such reason.** This is important, because Mike doesn't ask for anything but merely gives a friendly heads-up that somebody worth spending a few moments with might say hi.

The wrong way, which I hear over and over, is for the intermediary to tell the target, *"You need to meet So-and-So"* or *"Be sure to meet..."* Nobody in the spotlight or in a leadership role at an event needs an additional distraction or task to worry about. Instead, the person of interest should be told that there is someone who may make an approach and who that person is so the introduction will be expected.

In the absence of knowing people who know people, contact the host of the event and ask if he or she would make the introduction, if there's a moment. This is a perfectly reasonable request.

MAKE THE MOVE

Almost there. If you're nervous, take heart from knowing that your target may be secretly dying to be interrupted because he's been pinned by an artless interrupter or some other species of bore.

A glazed-over look is one of the signs that your time is now. You see it because you moved into non-invasive eavesdropping distance and waited for an opening, which might be as brief and fleeting as somebody taking a breath or sipping a beverage.

Be relaxed and natural as you move in.

Say "Excuse me for a second," as you smile and make eye contact with your target.

Have your hand out to shake at comfortable arm's length.

Say something super-fast and flattering about what an honor or thrill (or whatever) it is to meet and what a fascinating presentation (or whatever) and introduce yourself.

While this is happening, the target should be shaking your hand reflexively.

There you are, introduced and shaking. And the clock is ticking.

TICK TOCK

You have five seconds, no more, to turn reflexive courtesy into genuine welcome.

If you have one, you should already be trotting out your third-party prep, *"I believe Peyton Chan mentioned to you that I would introduce myself."*

Or maybe you built your own bridge in advance and can say something like, *"Excuse me, Governor. I'm Bill Unknown To You. Mayor Major Supporter told me to be sure to meet you and tell you about something we shared. And to pass on his best wishes."*

After the Gov says, *"Oh sure, how is that old rascal Mayor Major?"* or *"Peyton, what a force for change she is!"* and introduces you around, you have put some time back on your clock, but not much.

IN AND OUT

In a focused me-and-you moment of conversation with your target, say something worked out in advance that will pique interest and quickly get you to a specific outcome. The most practical goal is the go-ahead to communicate later.

> **You:** *Doctor Expert, we're going to be using some of your techniques in my business unit. Would you be interested in hearing about the results?*

> **Dr. Expert:** *Absolutely! I'd be more than interested.*

> **You:** *What's the best way to pass them on?*

Notice that your first question establishes your knowledge and interest leading to action. This is more flattering than "You're my hero!" and opens the door to future contact, as adulation does not.

As you pose your second and last question, pull out a card and pen or smartphone notes app and wait expectantly to take down an email address, name of a staffer, or other contact info.

Mission accomplished. After words of gratitude reflecting genuine excitement about making contact, you are good to go. And it's good to go at the next graceful and opportune moment. Leave the way you came, upbeat and with purpose.

You may have a long-term outcome in mind, but don't even think about pitching whatever it is. Your aim is to make a favorable first impression and permission for further contact.

PRACTICE, PRACTICE

The Good Lord must have wanted us to get really good at interpersonal skills, because he gave us billions of people to practice on! If you're in a room, and there are people in it, work the room, meeting and greeting, linking and syncing.

No-fail opener: "Hi, I'm Steve. What brings you here today?"

There's an old country-folk expression, "Dance with the one who brung you." Great for barn dances, I suppose, but no way to get the most out of a group. Break away from those who brung you or who you brung. Don't be like the timid ninety-nine percent who huddle in little friend groups. Approach people you've never met!

INTERRUPTION TYPE B: SPEAKING UP IN A MEETING

KNOW THYSELF

Always check yourself out before you chime in. To merit attention of others on the team, your contribution must be directly related to shared purpose and productive results. A need to be noticed, old scores to settle, and ego-tripping are <u>not</u> reasons to interrupt.

Be mindful, too, that words obey the Law of Supply and Demand. Keep the price of yours high by using them sparingly. Always speak to a purpose and stick to the point, and others will learn to listen and value what you say.

TECHNIQUE

Two letters to remember: **Cushion** and **Question**

The Cushion puts you on the same side as the person speaking. Even when you're in complete disagreement, focus on something just-said that you like and agree with so you're on common ground.

The Question is the most elegant and convincing way to lead others to the point you want to make. It lowers others' resistance and greatly lowers the risk of anybody losing face.

Let's say you're in a business something like mine, and your teammate Erin proposes promoting a seminar in Rochester. But you have experience and numbers that say it will be really hard to fill seats.

Instead of "No way," speak your Cushion: "I love Rochester. We've done things there before." And then the Question: "Erin, what do you like most about Rochester as a future target location?"

In subsequent back-and-forth, Erin and the team might re-think and reconsider, based on new input and discussion. But you never outright disagreed to get to this point.

YES, AND...

Even though you're not trying to be funny, there's a showbiz rule specific to unscripted comedy that applies: When you're ad-libbing, always agree with what the last person says. Go with it and build on it. Disagreement kills the comedy and the show. It isn't funny.

It really isn't funny if you don't Cushion but instead express adamant disagreement and end up looking like an idiot because you're wrong.

Imagine you're in a meeting planning an upcoming visit by Mr. Tetsuya Sato, head of Sato Corp in Osaka. This guy is a seriously huge deal with a lot in the works involving your company.

Your colleague Andy explains that he has arranged for Mr. Sato and some of your top leadership to go out for early dinner at Chuck E. Cheese's.

Inside you're screaming, "Kid pizza and arcade games and all that noise? Have you lost your mind?" but you stay calm and C-Q, saying how much your kids love that place or something like that and segue into a value-neutral Question: "Out of curiosity, what other options have we explored?" This is, by the way, a great question to ask when you believe somebody else is pushing a horrible idea. Your vibe is friendly, not confrontational, just asking to be filled in. But answering brings up other, saner alternatives and might save the day.

But surprise, surprise, Andy's choice turns out to be based on personal research. Sato Corp is about to launch a kiddie entertainment chain, and Mrs. Sato and the couple's four Chuck E. Cheese-age children are part of the entourage, seeing sights while he does business. They're dying to go!

Aren't you glad you used your head and did C-Q? To really be a hero at a meeting, you can C-Q to ask the question that everybody wants answered but hasn't figured out how to ask.

C-Q works every bit as well when you're in fundamental agreement with what's being said and want to get on-board, as in, "This is brilliant! What if we were to take it region-wide?"

SCHOOL RULE

Don't interrupt. If somebody else's mouth is open, you cannot open yours. If you don't have a clear go-ahead to join the conversation, keep quiet.

- LESSON FOR LIFE -

Interrupting is the only way you'll ever get to say anything! Get good at it. Then, when you need a moment of attention and chance to speak, step up and take it. Grownups are to be seen and heard!

9

DON'T BRAG

BUT EVERYBODY DOES NEED AN INTRODUCTION

For we who toil in the vineyards of public speaking and group presentations, being introduced comes with the territory. It's a welcome and worthwhile addition, and the intro can turn out to be great in its own right, like a killer concert warmup act.

I do have, however, have a bone to pick with certain introducers. Once in a while even good ones say *"Now, So-and-So needs no introduction..."*

Most introducers mean it as a compliment, but it's not. They have just done the speaker and themselves a disservice.

If there's no need, what in the world is this introducer doing up there now? On top of that, the more somebody supposedly doesn't need an introduction because he or she is so epically famous and important, the more you can count on warmup words of admiration and excitement.

The Truth: Everybody needs an introduction. The best introduction that can be had. Count this as another one of our Ultimate Truths. It applies to all of Life, miles away from rostrums and speakers' tables and audiences.

Setting yourself up to be properly introduced—so somebody else warms the audience up and gets them excited about you and your gifts and great things that will happen with you—is one of the greatest favors you can do for yourself and others. It's also the main point of this chapter.

The title *"Don't Brag"* has more of a mixed message than many of the old holdover lessons we set up and shoot down. It's both true and untrue. You absolutely have to brag. You must tell the world what it needs to know about you so it sits up and pays proper attention and respect. But here's the tricky part: You must brag without seeming to, in the most tactful, tasteful, dignified, appropriate, and credible manner. Then word about you becomes exciting information, not shameless self-aggrandizement and boastfulness.

You brag right by getting somebody else to do it for you. Then it isn't bragging at all—it's the introduction you need.

Picture a speaker, at the keynote presentation of a convention. She jumps up, cold, and starts throwing out things like...

"Okay, show of hands, how many out there have had the privilege of hearing from and learning from me and my amazing presentations before? If you've already had the pleasure, welcome back! You know what our first timers will soon know—that they're in for a truly peak encounter with a rare and memorable individual. You should be all be really excited! And feeling very fortunate, like my employees do, who will tell you why it's amazing to work with me in my organization that I founded from scratch. I am the embodiment of the American Dream!"

Creepy, even doing it ironically to make a point. But if somebody else got up and said it, nobody would bat an eye. Certainly nobody would judge the introducing speaker harshly for saying the words—as they surely would if the presenter spoke them herself.

There are natural laws beyond logic and linear cause-and-effect that govern how we think, feel, and behave. I have codified some of these Natural Laws of Behavior, and they're every bit as practical and effective in communication, organizational, and personal culture as Newtonian Physics are in mechanical engineering. Each chapter in my previous book, ***The Culture of Success***, lays out a Natural Law and shows exactly how to use it to build and maintain a positive, productive workplace culture.

There's a law at work right here—**The Law of Overhear Psychology**. We believe more what we overhear from others than what we hear directly. We credit information from a third party even when the person the information is about is present, like, say, a speaker standing next to the introducer. The same words about the same person can carry entirely different messages depending on who the words come from.

Overhear psychology rules, even at parties. Try this…

> **Scenario One:** *A giggly friend comes up and makes an intro—This is Bob, the guy I've been saying you have to meet. Is he gorgeous, or what?*

> **Scenario Two:** *No friend, just Bob—Hey there, you've got to meet me. Don't you think I'm gorgeous?*

First one could be flirty, fun, right? You might actually be glad to meet Bob. Same guy on his own in the second one? Run away!

WHACK-A-MOLE WITH LITTLE EGOS

Immutable Natural Laws are because they are. They're just how things operate. But in the human realm, Nurture counts as much as Nature. The myriad ways we think, feel, and behave are also shaped by outside circumstances and influences, especially by big people back when we were still little people. In this case, we were brought up to shun self-promotion, and we took the lesson as gospel.

The evidence is everywhere, in mature professionals who are absolutely loaded with native talent, training, experience, and skill. Do they shine like beacons, as they ought to? No, they try to disappear. As an old, very Texas mentor used to say, they couldn't lead a group in silent prayer. They're so humble, they say *"Excuse me,"* when they bump into a chair!

The problems start before kindergarten, sometime after potty training, which for many will be life's last experience in pure pride of accomplishment and unconditional praise. After that grownups start playing Whack-A-Mole with kids and their egos, encouraging them and making big happy fusses over accomplishments. But then Whack! they make sure Little Jimmy and Jilly never get too pleased with themselves and, heaven forbid, show and speak of it.

Mom and Dad are the original Ego Police and Brag Busters. How many ways did they tell us *"Don't brag"*? A dozen? A score? *"Don't toot your own horn." "Quit patting yourself on the back." "Don't get too big for your britches." "Who do you think you are?"* And on and on. The message, repeated hundreds of ways, thousands of times, was that there's something shameful and distasteful in telling others about your own best qualities, abilities, accomplishments.

This is worse than a lie. It's a catastrophe! Try to live by it, as millions do, and you're in deep trouble, not to mention deep you-know-what. Time and again, studies have shown that the greater measure of success in business is the ability to market oneself. By some measures this is fully eighty-five percent of success. Enthusiasm about you will do more than anything in the world to generate enthusiasm about what you have to offer the world.

NEVER FORGET THE SWEDISH ADMIRALS

This old tale may not be strictly factual, but it's full of truths. We have much to learn from it...

Admirals Sven and Olaf rose through the ranks faster than any naval officers in Swedish history, garnering every conceivable medal and honor. The King himself asked them to account for their amazing successes.

"Your Highness," said Admiral Sven, *"Admiral Olaf and I went to the naval academy together. Our backgrounds were humble, our families poor, while the other cadets were heirs to fortune and influence."*

"To make up for our lacks," said Admiral Olaf, *"we formed a pact to advance each other's causes."*

"Each time an officer commended me on a job well-done," Sven said, *"I'd tell him that I was merely following the example of Olaf."*

"Whenever a superior congratulated me on my knowledge, I'd tell him that Sven taught me," added Olaf.

"When the Commodore told me I was brave in battle, I said that I was inspired by Olaf."

"When I was wounded, I told how Sven carried me to safety."

"It should be clear, Sire," concluded Sven, "That the hero of this hour is really Olaf."

The other begged to differ, "The Champion of the Seas is Sven!"

The moral, which you already know: The most effective bragging is done by others.

You, like the Admirals, can make it happen by forming a bragging alliance and heaping praise on others while they do the same for you.

Sometimes, though, it's all on you. Time to get past "Don't Brag," once and for all.

RESULTS-PRODUCING THOUGHT AND ACTION

HOW TO BRAG WITHOUT SEEMING TO

- Be Your Own Swedish Admiral.

- Toot Your Own Horn, So Others Love The Tune.

- Being Bragged-About When You Have To Do It Yourself

D.I.Y. DILEMMA SOLVED.

Though good words from others are the uncontested Gold Standard of Bragging, we can't totally rely on them. The following how-to focuses on doing it yourself, which for many is profoundly uncomfortable even in concept, impossible face to face. Previous chapters cover techniques to reach out and make new contacts and leverage others' influence for your own benefit. These position you to approach others to say the right, good things about you.

WHY, WHY, WHY.

For whomever does the bragging/introducing on your behalf, the mission is the same—to generate up-front excitement and interest in you and what you have to offer.

Why the excitement? Well, because you matter. Which leads to three Why's...

- Why you?
- Why here?
- Why now?

Any introduction for any purpose should answer this question: *"Why should I listen to this particular person on this particular topic, at this particular time?"*

The Why's apply across the board, no matter if the intended intro/brag target is a single person learning about you in a phone call from an associate or email, or directly from you at an industry conference, where the answers to those Why questions tie in to why everybody's there. If, say, you're an independent screen producer at a gathering with potential major production partners and investors, you might matter because you've got a series in production, young talent coming on-board, and Silicon Valley money to fund new project development; and there is a big deal director and lead actor attached. You matter, because you're making things happen and you represent opportunity to people you meet.

In a purely social setting, the Why's skew social. At a wedding, it would matter that you're the groom's sister's boyfriend or you served with the groom in Iraq.

PUT THE WORDS INTO THEIR MOUTHS...

Speak with care and be mindful of messaging about you, because what people hear about you and pick up about you is generally what they repeat.

Exactly. And word for word.

Beware of False Modesty, the bane of Brag-aphobics, who reflexively mush-mouth, get jokey, and downplay what is and ought to be boast-worthy. Say what should be said straight. And play it straight.

Wrong: *Oh yeah, the award. I mean I was so surprised; I thought the committee must have made a mistake.*

Right: *I was so proud to be able to accept the award on behalf of the whole team. Definitely a high point for all of us.*

Note: The sharing of credit is always effective in artful bragging. It shows, without saying, very good things about you.

BRAGGING BACKWARD...

A high opinion of other people, a sincere fascination in their unique attributes and accomplishments, is a boomerang that does come back. The harder you throw it, the farther it goes, and the faster it comes winging back to you.

Four words to memorize: Be **interested**, not **interesting**!

Engage, and the other person will believe you're engaging. Laugh at the other guy's jokes, and he'll think you've got a great sense of humor. Be entertained, and show it, and the group will think you're a very entertaining person. And they'll share their opinion with still others. To sound sincere, and really keep the brag ball rolling, you must be sincere. This isn't hard at all, once you develop the habit of discovering others' praiseworthiness.

BRAG SURFING...

This is great to do at meetings and receptions. Great fun, too.

Start anywhere, with anybody. Introduce yourself, then make the other the person the star of the conversational show. Discover the subject dearest to his or her heart, and have fun talking about it. Ask questions. Be amazed by the answers.

After a while, bring in somebody else by introducing and bragging about your new acquaintance: *"Have you met Diane Jones? Well, you've got to! Diane is head of the research kitchen at Salty Snacks, and she's the one who invented spinach pretzels! They're absolutely huge! What were you telling me, Diane?"*

Tell enough people how they absolutely have to meet somebody else, and why, and sooner or later you're the person everybody has to meet.

LINK AND SYNC...

Get the hang of this, and you can say the most flattering things about yourself, no hint of the B-Word.

Open by asking questions and establishing commonalities— mutual acquaintances, business connections, places you've both been. Then, without taking the emphasis off the other person, start fishing that flow, throwing in little factual *"hooks"* about you. Watch for interest, and respond warmly to that interest, always reciprocating with more interest.

> **You:** *We've got really exciting new things going on with companies like yours, Charlie. By the way, I've been*

hearing some great things about your division. How long have you been running it?

Charlie: *About a year. What do you do with companies like ours?*

You: *We've had some great success, dramatically increasing sales and profit results.*

When Charlie bites, he'll want to know still more. Get him curious about you and asking questions, and he'll be much more impressed by what he pulls out of you, than any amount of self-promotion you push.

SCHOOL RULE

Don't brag. Nice folks don't do it. The hard-working and skillful don't have to. Self-promotion, in just about any form, is something to avoid.

- LESSON FOR LIFE -

Brag and get bragged about. You owe it to yourself and the world. Getting other folks to do it for you is best. If not, you've got to do it yourself.

10

TEACHER'S PET!
TEACHER'S PET!

SCHOOL OF BAD ATTITUDE

They get bigger, their voices change, and the vocabulary gets raunchier, so *"Teacher's pet!"* comes out all kinds of ways. But it's still the kids on Team Mediocre going *"Nyah Nyah"* when you show respect and make an effort to get along with higher-ups in your organization and show more productive results.

Could be that perceived proximity to the source of power makes others feel insecure and threatened, envious of rewards and recognition they're sure you will receive and they won't. Never mind that they, too, could step up and do better.

Who knows what's really happening with the going-nowhere crowd? More importantly, who cares?

If you keep it up and they keep it up they'll end up working for you. There's a t-shirt saying I like to quote to our Eagle U. students: NERD TODAY...BOSS TOMORROW. Funny, and too true.

A problematic relationship with authority figures is one of the areas where grownups can be most like grade-schoolers. But we weren't born with this *"Teacher's Pet!"* thing. We didn't even come to school with it. Most kindergartners adore their teachers and are eager to please, eager to learn. Within a few years, though, fledgling Turkeys have formed a flock and found their voices, making all sorts of derisive noise. They do everything they can to embarrass and stigmatize those who cultivate a relationship with the grownup who can do most for learning. They're denigrating the whole point of school.

Of course Teacher isn't the only authority figure. Down the hall sits Principal, a walking, talking Criminal Justice System. Even good kids who never get in trouble fear being sent to the Principal's office.

> Between the peer group jeering *"**Teacher's Pet,**"* and the dread of Principal, we've got a system that punishes those who try to maintain a constructive personal relationship with immediate authority figures and instills terror of more remote higher-ups.

These are attitudes to lose while you focus on where and how you want to get your strokes. You can earn approval from successful individuals who run things, who can show you the way and advance your cause. Or you can gobble *"Nyah Nyah!"* with the Turkeys.

Your choice.

UPSIZING THE SELF

The mere presence of powerful figures can bring on a shaky and helpless condition I call Authority Tremor. If you're part of a large organization, picture yourself alone in an elevator with the CEO. Would you feel relaxed and natural? Would you smile and say hello?

Chances are you would not, and the elevator ride would feel awkward in the extreme. There's no earthly, sensible reason why this should be so. After all, you have a lot in common. You both work toward the success and greater glory of the same organization, which relies on you both. You're equal before the Law. God loves you equally. Still, though, the lifetime of authority phobia is hard to leave behind.

> Step One is a bit of mental reprogramming.
> **You need to change your size. Get BIG.**

Don't laugh, it's true. Once upon a time we were literally little, and the people in charge were literally big. We all carry an atavistic sense of smallness that authority figures can revive, causing us to feel and even behave as if we were still knee-high.

Getting Big means giving yourself stature, taking up your own space. All contacts with everybody, even with your board president, founder, and owners, are eyeball-to-eyeball, grownup-to-grownup. Sure, others may have greater power over your professional destiny than you have over theirs. They have trappings of power like corner suite offices, company-leased cars, and use of the corporate jet.

But what they have does not diminish you, not in any way.

Getting Big, vis-a-vis authority figures, also means tuning out those who want to shame you out of having constructive, mutually respectful relationships with the people in charge. The nay-sayers try to sound bold and rebellious. They're merely giving themselves comfort and excuses not to grow up.

But it takes more than the right attitude to forge productive relationships with higher-ups. It takes insight, forethought, planning, and verbal skill. Like ninety-nine percent of thought and action that yields desired results, it requires a systematic approach. Learn the system, work it, and it will take you from a comfortable and natural opener to a team leader.

"Hey Charlene, got a minute?" An opener like that puts you on the path to career advancement and greater personal and financial rewards. You'll position yourself to ask for and get

good things only leadership can provide: more responsibility, recognition, promotion, and, yes, maybe even a raise. Who doesn't want that last one? Who knows how to ask for and get it, with low stress and maximal chances of a Yes?

You will after you read the following.

RESULTS-PRODUCING THOUGHT AND ACTION

A Guide to Getting Along with Those in Charge
- Your Fail-Safe System to Get Ahead and Stay Ahead

TRUTHS OF THE MATTER

Upon This Rock Stand Firm

There's only one solid foundation for building a productive, positive relationship with leaders: Do the best job you can with a continuing commitment to achieve ever better results for your team and the whole organization.

If this strikes you as idealistic, goody-goody, Teacher's Pet-ish, think again. It's stone-cold real-world truth and solid strategy for self-advancement.

Don't Curry Favor, Earn It

He or she who tries to make a favorable impression on higher-ups without delivering the goods and earning true approval is a suck-up, a variety of Turkey you do not want to be. Everything, for such a person, is manipulation and bluff. Sooner or later reality—often in the form of a savvy leader who sees right through it—calls the bluff. Though *"Nyah-Nyah!"* Turkeys find it hard to believe, it's also easier and less stressful to dig in and do a job you're proud of.

Shared Vision—It's On You to Get It

What you really need to get about your position and responsibilities, which leadership expects you to get, you may not get at all because nobody tells you what success and a job well done look like.

Theoretically speaking, it's leadership's responsibility to communicate shared vision and specific results for which you are responsible. Practically speaking, however, you must make sure it happens.

For any number of reasons, leader(s) may be desperately in need of help here. You help yourself by helping them. The unshared vision is the greatest cause of superior-subordinate troubles. And trouble always tends to flow downhill, to you, with potentially deleterious effects on your reputation and prospects. If trouble gets out of hand, it can cost you your job.

Fully Baked and Out of the Oven

This you must absolutely ask for and get: a crystal-clear understanding and grasp of specific results for which you are responsible.

BEWARE OF NARROW TASK-MINDEDNESS

Performing a task does not equal a result.

Let's say, as a simple example, that you're on the staff of a medical or dental practice and routinely take calls from new and current patients. Answering the phone is on your task list, but the immediate desired result is an appointment on the books. The ultimate result, which you help lock in with a positive attitude and verbal skills, is a patient who will keep the appointment, continue care, and refer others to this terrific practice.

Keep the Purpose in Mind

There's no need to visit and revisit the organization's high-level purpose in regular communication. But you must keep it in mind to create and maintain your Personal Culture of Success. And for immediate success, you've got to know the results that count most for your immediate leader(s). Here, again, you may have to take the lead, be proactive, and ask.

Get the Picture, Fast

Vital communication on a day-to-day basis likely involves small- and middle-size portions of the big picture, involving things that need to happen near-future, which you can make happen.

Think through an issue where you feel you need clarity, and try a sentence like, *"If I understand you right, Bernie, we now need to set up that warehousing in Buffalo by May 15, not June 15. Is that right?"* That, and a couple of follow-ups should establish, in no more than ninety seconds, what's on Bernie's mind. The question at the end is important, because a *"Yes"* signals understanding and a clear go-ahead to action. Get permission to give updates on progress and results.

If you don't see the picture, don't pretend you do. Ask, don't guess.

YOUR BIG 3 NEED TO KNOWS

A productive, positive, and mutually satisfactory relationship depends on sure knowledge of three things:

1. **Big picture goals**

2. **Leadership's strong likes**

3. **Leadership's strong dislikes**

If, say, you have a new person in charge, you can cover the ground in easy, natural-seeming questions like:

"What I'd like to find out is this: What are three or four of the most important things for me and my team to make happen?"

"Could you tell me about some of your strongest preferences?"

"With the same honesty, could you tell me a few of the things that really get on your nerves, so my people and I can avoid them?"

You will, of course, use your own words and adapt yourself to the flow of the conversation. But if you nail this stuff down, you'll have a hard time screwing things up.

With current leadership, you can stay in sync with an annual re-do. Ask for a report card, listen, act on it, and get permission to follow up. Find out what's really wanted with our favorite blue-sky line: *"If you had a magic wand, and could wave it to get whatever you wanted here, what would it be?"*

General Points

Focusing on results de-personalizes the relationship and puts the shared emphasis where it belongs. It keeps things comfortable and clear.

Enthusiasm

Make superior(s) know you appreciate them, without seeming like a suck-up, by appreciating the work and results. When you get a kick out of something, show it.

HOW TO GET AHEAD AND STAY AHEAD IN YOUR CAREER

The Universal Formula for Communication with Leader(s)

To Take Responsibility for Career Success, Advancement, Satisfaction, and Compensation, Lead Your Own Personal Cultural Revolution!

Believe It

We've seen the system work way too often not to believe. One client was absolutely bowled over when his organization's CEO gave him a huge promotion to a position several levels above his current position. All he had done, basically, was ask, *"How will you know that I'm the best person in this position you've ever had?"* The leader said, *"Let me get back to you on that."* He never did get back, but then word came down about the client's promotion, which was unprecedented in the company.

Why It Works

This approach will work because it relies on the Law of Compensation: Give more, and you get more. This is one of the most powerful principles in business. You are in the business of advancing your organization's cause and bottom line in profits or other performance metrics. He or she who earns more for the organization eventually gets more. *"Eventually"* comes more quickly and surely when you position yourself to ask for more and get it.

Game On

It all starts with a plan to address a situation within your current areas of responsibility, where you see a way to achieve better results.

When you have something in mind, ask for a few minutes to discuss some things you've noticed and ideas you want to get feedback on.

Describe the situation in question and segue into possible action to take, delivered as a question.

Situation:	Question:
"When we receive incoming orders, it takes us hours to keep them straight and get them processed."	*"Has anybody thought of trying XYZ? Do you think that would work?"*

Frame the solution as a question so you don't front yourself as the problem solver. This avoids any implication of overstepping bounds. You're respecting the lines of authority and sharing ownership of potentially valuable outcomes. Get permission to give updates on progress. Do it as directly and quickly as you can.

Build On It

Your call whether to build on your win with another for positive momentum. Or, if it's a big win and you're sharing excitement about it, you could be ready for bigger questions for the leader and bigger answers for you.

Positioning and Setup

"I'm really excited about what we're achieving here, and would love to build on it."

"I want you to know that I really want to do more for the organization and grow with it, and take on more responsibility."

"What other ways do you see that I can be of more value to the company?"

What You Said Without Saying

You just asked for an advancement, and indications that if you keep it up you can rise higher. You also flattered and showed respect and gratitude to the higher-up, recognizing her or his role in your success.

Bad News Can Be Good, Too.

After all this, the right kind of leader is going to say, *"Bring it on!"* conspicuously, volubly thrilled to discover enthusiasm, ability, aligned interests, and maybe a new star.

Unfortunately, you can't count on having the right kind of boss or organization with growth opportunities. You can, however, do yourself worlds of good by recognizing when interests do not align and there may be no path to advancement.

Seeing a dead end sign can get you promotions and raises, too. They'll be in your new job in a dynamic organization where your star will shine.

HOW NOT TO GET A RAISE OR ANYTHING ELSE

A: Say You're Overdue

"I've been working here for XXX years."

The message here is that the company owes you just for putting in time. A sense of entitlement is career poison. Don't even say this sort of thing to yourself.

B: Cry Poor

"Everything's been going up. We're barely making ends meet..."

It may be true, but tell a higher-up you're in financial trouble at home, and you cast doubt on yourself. If you can't manage your own resources, why on Earth should the company rely on you, much less give you greater responsibility and compensation?

SCHOOL RULE
Big folks in charge are the enemy.
Try to please and get along
with them and you're a suck-up,
disloyal to peers and self.

– LESSON FOR LIFE –
Higher-ups are exactly the
people you want to get along
with. Do everything you can—
except sucking-up—to exceed
the standards set by those in
charge. The more you do for
them, the more they're going
to do for you!

CAN I GO TO THE BATHROOM?

WELL, __CAN__ YOU?

Join me as we journey back together to Beacon Heights Elementary to honor my fifth-grade teacher, Mrs. Gibbs. She taught us some valuable lessons by answering the bathroom question like this:

"I don't know, can you?"

The joke was partly an English lesson. *"May I?"* is, of course, the correct way to ask for permission. The dictionary says that **can** is a matter of ability.

But this was also a larger lesson. Mrs. Gibbs was, in her humorous way, teaching us that we'd reached an age and level of self-control where pitstops can be taken care of in regularly scheduled breaks. It's your business so see to it yourself in your own time, Mrs. Gibbs was saying. Thus she took this particular Teacher-student permission off the table.

Happily, this bathroom thing was pretty well settled. I do seminars and presentations all over the world, and no one so far has raised a hand and asked the B Question. (Considering the acute, emergency cases of Inner Kindergartner Syndrome out there, I wouldn't be so surprised if somebody does.)

PRISONERS OF PERMISSION

Meanwhile, in vitally important areas involving success, happiness, health, and wealth, millions of grownups are trapped in grade school, hands in the air, waiting for somebody else to give them permission to do what they ought to do. In the absence of a clear go-ahead from somebody else, they wait while their best ideas languish, opportunities pass by, and hopes and dreams wither. They don't achieve and live the way they want to, because NOBODY SAYS IT'S OK!!!

How on Earth did we get this way? Well, we were trained into it. Before we get to school we live and breathe permission under a permanent, across-the-board regimen of needing to ask somebody big before doing practically anything under threat of yelling and time outs for doing it without permission. As ever with lessons to be unlearned now, Rule by Permission made perfect sense for children, especially young children, who need close monitoring and supervision. Denying your pre-K twins permission to let go of your hand and clamber around at the rim of the Grand Canyon like it's a playground is not helicopter parenting and control freakiness. You're using situational awareness and judgment that the kids completely (and happily) lack. Thanks to you and parental permission, they'll live to enter kindergarten.

In early schooling, Teacher permission continues to promote safety as well as crowd control and general good order. Then, all the way through post-doc fellowships, we are gears in a great big Permission Machine. Think back; you'll hear Teacher saying, *"Don't turn over the test and start writing until I give the signal."* *"No talking unless I call on you."* It never stopped.

University and professional degrees, education's ultimate symbols of attainment, are great big letters of permission, signed by Teacher (as embodied in faculty committees and review boards). A diploma is nothing but a Hall Pass for the World! It gives us permission to go to previously off-limits places and do new and exciting things.

ESCAPING THE COMFORT ZONE

Reluctance, doubt, disbelief, fear—when you're starved for permission, these are the hunger pangs. Like real chronic hunger, chronic lack of permission dulls you and saps your will. Eventually you stop feeling hungry, and denying yourself permission—even when it's there for the taking—becomes reflexive and a source of comfort. People build whole worlds for themselves with walls and fences that don't exist. Call it the Comfort Zone. It's a big part of life to get out of that zone and stay out.

How can you tell when you're trapped in your Comfort Zone? For one thing, you're way too comfortable, but it's a joyless, dull sort of comfort, which is all about avoiding discomfort. You pay a high price to live in the Comfort Zone. Costs of lost opportunity, in financial and personal rewards foregone, are astronomical. Inner utility bills keep going up because of the effort it takes to make reality always say, *"No, you can't."* Anything that could get you out of the Comfort Zone becomes a threat, and people go to amazing lengths to try to make the Comfort Zone homier. They join the Turkey Flock, shun the company of people they really admire, and give up on their fondest dreams for themselves and loved-ones.

But not trying is in the end always more painful, exhausting, and costly than trying. It's the hell on Earth described by Thoreau when he wrote, *"The masses of men lead lives of quiet desperation."*

PERMISSION GRANTED

So where do you get your energizing, go-ahead, green light capital P-Permission?

You must give **yourself** permission!

Easy, right?

Not necessarily.

"Give yourself permission…" is one of the most oft-spoken, all-purpose, glib, feel-good things to say in self-help and pop psych. Nobody has not heard it, possibly dozens of times in any number of situations, like giving yourself permission to break the bounds of the possible and be the fire-breathing colossus of success you really are or permission to pop for an upgrade to a poolside suite on vacation or whatever.

Like a lot of popular feel-good stuff, *"Give yourself permission,"* manages to be both perfectly true and pretty much useless, because it's not clear how to put it in action and get results.

It's true that you need to provide your own permission. At this stage of life, who else can you count on to provide it? This makes even more sense, because you're very likely the one withholding it.

But high-powered, results-producing permission comes from both within and without. The trick, rather than simply self-gifting, is to make changes so your whole world says, *"Yes, you can! Of course you may!"* and *"What are you waiting for?"*

The real truth, properly expressed, would be more like *"**Get yourself** permission."* Not quite as easy and instant-feel-good to stand up and shout, but much better because it works!

Permission is all over, though it often isn't immediately recognizable as permission. Seek and you will find all you need. So will anybody else who does the following.

RESULTS-PRODUCING THOUGHT AND ACTION

PERMISSION HUNT

Ultimate Letter of Permission

This one is a gift that you make to yourself. Write out your major life-defining goal and a runner-up goal or two on a notecard or something durable about that size. Look at it every single day and carry it with you the way you carry a driver license and credit cards.

You may be tempted to do a phone note or some kind of digital reminder that's also ever-present physically and instantly accessible, but we have found that tech alone doesn't cut it. For years I have spoken and written on the power of written-down goals to focus effort and ultimately achieve those goals. The point right here is that you're also giving yourself permission. Who says it's okay to think and dream big and start working toward achieving those dreams? You do, and you have it in writing. In your own hand writing.

A goal grants permission—double-whammy permission, actually—in that it denies you permission to wait around because nobody told you to go ahead. Keep in mind that you take many steps to reach your big goal(s). Map out short-term intermediary goals on the way to big ones, and know that you already have built-in blanket permission to achieve them all.

Person-to-Person Permission

A Mentor is much more than an invaluable source of information, inspiration, and personal encouragement from somebody who knows more of what you need to know and who has reached levels of experience and success to which you aspire. A mentor is permission in human form. What is encouragement, if not permission to do more and do it better from someone you deeply admire? Once again, this is turbo-charged permission, because the mentor/protégé relationship denies permission to aim lower and do less.

Peer-to-peer works, too. Pick somebody you respect, admire and, above all, trust, and tell them about a goal you'd love to get going on now. If something holds you back, talk about what it might be. Commit to make a strong start toward your goal, with the clear understanding that you want to keep getting together to talk about your progress. Say, *"This is so great! I'd love to do the same thing for you."*

We sometimes call such a mutual support duo Accountability Partners. Permission Partners would apply just as well. With a mentor or partner, you get solid, platinum Permission. Just by listening and nodding, somebody else can green light your aspirations. You can return the favor. Make it a habit to inspire others, to set them free of whatever's holding them back. Never forget to say how much you appreciate others' interest and support and get permission to keep the relationship going and to continue checking in.

You don't have to say *"Permission"* to ask for and get it. *"Is it okay with you if..."* or *"Would you mind...."* say it better in normal conversation without sounding like you're back in school.

BOOBY-TRAP GUILT

It's especially important to communicate with those closest to you whose lives may be affected by changes you make, so they get what's up and hopefully provide a go-ahead. For example, knowing you're pushing toward a big new goal can ease potential strain between you and your spouse, who might otherwise be hurt by your longer hours and intense concentration. *"I wanted you to understand and know that it is okay with you"* can work wonders.

Staying in-sync, with life partner permission, defuses the guilt bomb. It's hard for sensitive, decent people to believe it's okay to hurt other people. Maybe your concern is that your kids feel neglected because you're around less and are preoccupied. Or you just feel guilty about making changes and rising higher and don't know why. Like a real booby-trap, guilt can be tricky to figure out and disarm; there are tripwires every which way. Make sure you know what you're looking at, and remember that guilt can also be a wonderful excuse for those who don't really want change. They can stay in the Comfort Zone and admire themselves for sparing others' feelings.

Remember, too, that some people around you, even close to you, will never be okay with you changing and achieving new success. Same-level peers may like you, but some may not be cool with your breakout moves. If the really envious could stop you by denying you permission, they would. Short of that, they telegraph disapproval and try to make you uncomfortable. Comfort Zone lifers are especially good at guilt-tripping. But that guilt is in your head. If somebody else came in and planted it, you gave them permission.

WEARABLE PERMISSION

It's far easier to get to the next level and be accepted and respected if you look like you belong. Upgrade your clothes, grooming, posture, physique. Take the trauma out of buying up and working out by calling it an investment, as it is. What does this have to do with permission? A lot. People often say OK, automatically, to those who look OK for where they are, like they fit in. Wherever you want to go, there's a dress code: *No shirt. No shoes. No service.* Most of the time, the codes aren't posted on signs. But they're there. This is for you, too. It's easier to give yourself the go-ahead when you look in the mirror and see Success.

COMPANY YOU KEEP

Yes, we're back to flying with the Eagles and tuning out Turkeys. The former give us permission to soar high by soaring themselves. They love to fly high with their own kind. The latter want you to stay on the ground and gobble.

By the way, you don't need to be snotty about Turkeys. Nobody gave you permission to be a jerk. But you can cancel other people's permission to mess around with yours.

High achievers give others permission to achieve by achieving. All the air goes out of *"I can't"* in the presence of a person who says out loud or by example, *"I can, and the proof is I did. Now why can't you?"* People you'll never meet, who are thousands of miles away or dead for thousands of years and possibly mythic, can provide permission for you to break out and do huge new things.

This far into the book, I give myself permission to stop here, because I am sure you get it. The Permission you seek awaits. The right people want to give it to you.

WORDS OF WARNING

When you say to yourself *"Stop! Don't, that's impossible!"* give yourself a listen at least for a minute. Not all self-permission deficiencies are all in your head. Impossible can be, you know, impossible, and hesitation and fear hold you back from wasting resources on futility or even deadly danger. Sometimes you've got to be your own grownup, refusing to let go of your own hand so you don't run around and fall off a cliff. Sometimes you must to say, *"No, I don't give myself permission."* You don't want to tune out and ignore yourself.

SCHOOL RULE

Wait for permission. It's not OK
until somebody says it's OK.

- LESSON FOR LIFE -

Don't wait for permission,
but just go get it! Make
what you want to do OK by
getting permission from
others and the whole wide
world to do the things you
want to do. Your big, go-
ahead green light is shining!

12

WAIT FOR THE BELL

RING, RING

B ack in the schoolhouse, Time had a face: the clock on the wall. And it had a voice: an earsplitting electric bell. We learned to tell Time, but Time really did all the telling to us.

RING! Time to be in your seats.

RING! Time to go down the hall to the music room.

RING! Lunch time.

RING! Time to get the heck away from school and the bell.

The clock and bell pushed us through the day, telling us precisely what to do minute by minute. Famished and with your stomach growling like a Rottweiler in a bad mood, you still had to wait for lunch time, when everybody ate whether hungry or not. Why? That was lunch time, not just lunch. Did Miss Pedagog, back in kindergarten, tell us to start gulping milk and crunching cookies because we seemed to be in the mood? No, it was milk and cookie time. Time, time, time. No matter how much you were in the mood to do some addition and subtraction, you had to wait until it was time for arithmetic. Academics later became periods as much as subjects. School even had a time crime—tardiness—that could earn repeat offenders a trip to Principal's office.

Home was school all over. Mama didn't yell, *"Smothered pork chops, potatoes and peas!"* No, it was *"Supper time!" "Time to come indoors!" "Time for your paper route."* And on and on. What did we learn from all this? A great many things, some of them absolutely necessarily. A consciousness of time and conscientiousness about it is a baseline necessity for civilized human beings. Everybody doing whatever they want, whenever they want, equals chaos. Schools can't run that way. Nor can families, businesses, or society in general.

This far into the book, you know it's time to get hit with the downside of all this time training. Here it is: We grow up in great peril of becoming permanent clock-aholics and bell addicts. Oversized, overaged kids watching the clock instead of their work and their lives, and talking to themselves the way Teacher and Mom and Dad used to, with focus on the time instead of actions and results.

- Starting time
- Quitting time
- Break time
- Vacation time
- Time for the annual raise
- Promotion
- Retirement

The scheduling is much more complicated and spans decades, but it's grade school all over again.

Time management was my first seminar topic when I first began presenting. I quickly realized how many people let the clock make a mess out of them. I still deal with casualties of the clock. Some don't start doing what they ought to, because they don't know if it's time to start. Some quit too soon, just because it's quitting time.

Many are still prisoners of the forty-hour workweek. They fail to realize their ambitions because they're limited by the nine-to-five. Others don't know when to quit. The eighty-hour-a-week zombies are too worn out to enjoy the fruits of their labors and their family lives are in shambles (if they still have families). Individual symptoms are all over the board, but the root cause is the same: These folks never learned to put time to work for them. Instead, they work for it and watch the clock, because otherwise they wouldn't know what to do.

It's time to get on top of time, which doesn't leave us any middle ground. If you don't make it your friend, it's your enemy. If you're not managing it, it's your boss. If you're not in control, you're in chaos.

ORGANIZING PRINCIPLE

This need to beat the clock so it quits beating on us has spawned multibillion-dollar industries. It used to be all about clever calendars and organizers. Now software and phone apps tell us what we're supposed to be doing and who we are supposed to be doing it with at every moment. Digital notifications are the present-day school bell:

DING! Time to read the news.

DING! Time to read an e-mail.

DING! Time to go to the meeting.

DING! Time to read a text message.

DING! Time to pick up the package that was just delivered.

DING! Time to look at your social media because someone just tagged you in a photo.

DING! Time to look at the security camera because someone just rang your door bell at home.

DING!

DING!

DING!

Your time is not your own. It's a wonder anyone gets anything done.

But there's one thing written or digital organizing tools can't do. They can't organize you. There's a missing element, which no third-party system can supply. Without this element, you're just creating your own techy clocks and bells and letting them chase you through the day. True, such tools can be a great help, but they function on a shallow level. They're merely timetables, not dynamic, proactive organizers of precious hours and minutes. We need a deeper organizing principle.

The Bible, the ultimate self-help book and guide to success, tells us what it is:

> *To every thing there is a season, and a time to every purpose under heaven*

(Ecclesiastes 3:1, KJV).

If the Prophets wanted to teach us grade-school rules, they would have written

To repeat, *A Time to Every Purpose.*

There's a Purpose to Every Time.

That, basically, is what Teacher and the other grownups used to tell us when they announced lunch time, break time, play time, and on and on.

Knowing what you ought to be doing at any particular moment becomes clear as a Colorado trout stream when you know why. And all your little, everyday why's become brighter and clearer when they're part of a great big WHY that is your Purpose. This is Why you're living and Why you're doing what you're doing.

Get straight with your major, defining, ultimate purpose. Revisit it. You'll probably discover you're dealing with a few, because there are intermediate goals on the way to the ultimate.

Every day, bright and early, invest some time going over your personal purpose and vision. Note, please, that we're not talking about a to-do list. This is more of a **TO-BE** list. It expresses who you are and what you intend to do with your life.

Hold on, what am I hearing out there? If you are in the middle of a perceived Time Crisis, you are saying, *"But I'm too busy for that. I don't have time to do that."*

Think again—You don't have time not to!

Know yourself and your purpose, and the time becomes much more manageable. You still have to schedule and plan, but it will come much more easily, with less stress and conflict. Time will be on your side.

RESULTS-PRODUCING THOUGHT AND ACTION

CHECK THE TIME

Answer the following completely. *"Because it was time to"* is NOT an acceptable response.

- When did you get up this morning? Why? Why did you get up when you got up?

- What time did you go to lunch? Why? Were you hungry? Why did you spend as much time as you did at lunch?

- When did you go home from work? Why just then, and not sooner or later?

- Ask the same when/why questions at all important junctures of the day: Why now? Why this?

- Inasmuch as it's feasible, given practical considerations and limits, adjust how you use time until you like your answers to the previous questions better.

- Be on time; in fact, be early, but make it count by being on purpose.

- Zoom back to ultimate life purposes. Remind yourself who you are, to what ultimate purpose.

- Tick tock.

Let's dip back into the Old Testament, reading deeper into the third chapter of the Book of Ecclesiastes. After the first verse, Solomon tells us there's a time to be born and time to die, to plant, to reap, to laugh, and to cry; he adds that there are times for physical loving, for abstaining, for winning, and for losing. As is usual in Biblical verses, there's wisdom for living here as well as beauty.

Ecclesiastes draws no lines between life's times and purposes. Everything gets mixed-up: personal issues, work, citizenship, material gain, and loss. We have but one allotted time to live, which intermingles all these things.

Modern thinking (or lack thereof) says to compartmentalize and do the opposite, to try to live separate lives that rarely or never meet. The way we speak shows the tendency, for we label them professional life, home life, love life, family life. Such talk can seem hard-edged and sensible, and it helps us define what we want to accomplish in each area of life. But the reality is we have ONE life and we're living it no matter where we are and what we're doing. We can't get into it or out of it, closer, or farther.

Pretend that You the Professional Person are somebody different from You the Mother of Three, You the Daughter, the Aunt, the Sunday School Teacher, the Co-Vice-President of the PTA, and on and on. This is a formula for irresolvable internal conflict and turmoil. Every choice about what to do and when is zero-sum win-lose. Do more at work, you're more of a Professional, less of a Husband, Father, Son, Neighbor. Leave a convention a day early so you can watch your daughter swim in the state finals, and Dad You takes a big piece out of Professional You.

You'll never take all the conflict out of personal scheduling. This world of ours is too demanding and hurried for that. But there's a key that clarifies and simplifies the whole business: Remember who makes the decisions. It's You who is more than the sum of the roles you play in life. Be inclusive, not exclusive. Always you, all the time. You and your purpose are the bell, not your different roles and responsibilities.

This doesn't mean performing all your roles at once. If, say, you're a mother and federal prosecutor, you can't play with the little ones while making opening arguments in court. But it's critically important to make both roles part of the harmonious whole You. Doing your professional best to see that justice is served is a way to love your family, by doing what you do with excellence and purpose. The fact that you have a family also can make you better at your job. The roles don't oppose unless you place them in opposition. Play them in combination, and you'll play them all better.

No one can tell you what your Purpose in Life is or ought to be. But you need to know what it is. And you need to remind yourself of it every single day.

Do it, and you'll know what to do with your days—and your hours, minutes, and seconds— instead of Time telling you what to do. **RING. RING. DING!**

SCHOOL RULE
Wait for the bell. Live by the clock. You know, by the date, hour, and minute what you ought to be doing and for how long.

- LESSON FOR LIFE -
Be on Purpose, and you'll be on time. Know who you are, what you're doing, and why you're doing it, and you'll know much more about what to do with your time. You are the bell.

13

Won't Mommy and Daddy Be Proud?

DON'T COUNT ON IT

For your own good, don't depend on it, either.
Seriously.

We all crave recognition, appreciation, and acknowledgement.
All of us!

It starts early. *"Mom, look at me!"* *"Dad. Dad. Dad. Watch me!"*
And then later in life, who is the first person mentioned when
the world is watching? Even professional football players say
it on T.V. *"Hi, Mom!"*

In study after study of workplace motivation and satisfaction, recognition is consistently ranked as one of the top motivators. We all want it. We all need it.

But what happens when you don't get the recognition you want from the sources you are expecting? From Mom and Dad, other family members, friends, or your employer? Leave recognition to the random whims of others, and you will frequently be disappointed.

Some of the highest achievers in the world have a painful void in their lives because they feel they never got the recognition they thought they deserved from Mom or Dad. On the other hand, under achievers never reach their potential because they never got the encouragement or recognition they felt they needed.

Both ways there's a price to pay for what is, at the root, the same problem, which is playing to the wrong audience. Either it's:

- An audience that may not understand or like the show being performed, or
- The people in the crowd love a show that does more for them than the star.

Among the self-evident truths about Life, there's this:

Life is a performance.

Whoever we are, whatever we do, we're in show biz. The people watching the show may be mostly or altogether in our heads, but nevertheless we knock ourselves out for their approval. And if we fail to make a positive connection, we suffer for it.

Think about the people feeling permanently let-down and aggrieved because they crave the approval they never got from parents, family, or whomever they decided was the audience they needed to please. What are the odds of a brand-new burst of pride and a standing ovation from the *"crowd"* who has constantly let them down? You're right, not good. If they haven't done it in the past, it's not likely they will do it in the future. After a full performance, an unenthusiastic audience is not likely to change its attitude.

The solution starts where the problems reside. In the head. That's where the inner audience sits and where the *"Please me!"* tape started running very early on.

For little kids, the first, primal audience is usually Mom and Dad. Theirs is the original gold-standard approval that many still seek. By kindergarten, they've been joined by Teacher and classmates and then we have three Ps—parents, peers, and professors—to perform for and please.

Peers become more and more important to good or bad effect. For vulnerable or at-risk teens, bad company is a destructive tyranny and pleasing the wrong peers a flat-out disaster. Even when the susceptible are all alone, jerks in the imaginary front-row seats egg them on and get them in trouble.

But the growing-up years bring another change that is fundamental and truly life-altering:

You choose your audience!

We possess the freedom to change the people for whom we perform and can therefore put on the hit shows of our dreams, to thundering applause.

YOUNG EAGLES

We hammer this home at Eagle U, our weeklong, intensive summer programs to jumpstart success for high school and college students. Young people are challenged to look deep and think about who they are really performing for and trying to please versus who they really ought to be trying to please.

A genius member of our Eagle U faculty, Pam Peterson, makes this an Eagle U high point, turning it into an invaluable exercise about participants' own shows. They all look within and visualize themselves onstage. Then they fill the empty seats with people who applaud for them, people whose attention and recognition bring out their absolute best to spur them on to even better.

Part of the exercise is tell-yourself-the-truth time: Who's really in your crowd now? What pleases them, earns their applause? Do they get you and your aspirations, reward you for exceeding expectations, or do they hoot and holler for mediocrity? The questions often lead to Truth, Part 2: Time for an audience upgrade.

We make it unmistakably clear that this is much more than a thought problem with theoretical answers. What's at stake is nothing less than life—**your** life—how you live it and what you do with it for your own benefit and the world's.

The audience you try to please controls your **entire life**.

RESULTS-PRODUCING THOUGHT AND ACTION

YOUR AUDIENCE

Here's an Eagle U assignment for anyone. Look and think deep when answering...

- Who's in my audience now?
- What do I do to try to please them and get applause?
- Do I get cheers for doing my best at what I want to be best at?
- Does my audience settle for mediocrity or do they cheer for excellence?
- If I'm playing to the wrong audience, who do I want up front who will understand me and cheer me on to bigger and better performances?

Visualize your own performance space. You stand on stage and pick members of your ideal audience and place them, one by one, exactly where you want them. Put the best people in the best seats to see you do your best, appreciate your performance and cheer for you.

Remember: You're filling your seats with individuals who are ideal for you and your dream performance.

Though this chapter begins with words of caution about depending on approval from Mom and Dad, it could be that one or more close family members truly belong in your audience. Shortly I'll tell you a bit about my own father and his role in my personal audience. He's not the only family member present. In my writing, I strive to favorably impress and honor the legacy of my great-grandfather. Why? Well, he was an amazing writer, and his legacy inspires me.

I share these examples to help free up your thinking about who you put in your audience. The more you think, the more obvious it becomes who you want and why.

Whenever I speak in front of a group, Bill Gove has a seat of honor on the front row. Bill, a legendary leader and teacher of professional speakers, was the first president of the National Speakers Association. Early in my career, he was generous enough to sit in my seminar audience for a day and then spend the entire next day giving me a marathon session of line-by-line, action-by-action coaching and instruction that ranks among my most intense days of learning I have ever had. I was never the same.

Bill has since passed on, but he's still there watching and listening and inspiring me to be worthy of his approval. I benefit hugely as does my audience, because I knock myself out to do my best.

D.I.Y. FAMILY THERAPY

To reiterate, it may be that your ideal inner audience does not include Mom or Dad. If so, giving their VIP seats to somebody else may seem terribly wrong. Ditto leaving out other close family members and beloved home folks who used to clap when you baby-burped and came to your school plays and track meets.

Old ties are deep and dear. You can and should honor and cherish—and love–your people. But you should also keep your feelings where they belong and honor your own ambitions.

Here's your guilt-free fix, starting with Mom and Dad: Let them be Mom and Dad. Love them no matter how they react to what you do. Stop wanting them to be an ideal audience that they may never be. They gave you what they could when you were young. They're doing the best they can now.

As a fellow adult, show some understanding. You may move into territory completely foreign to them that seems threatening. As you go beyond their Comfort Zone and they see you taking risks, they may also become protective. Their deep, primal—parental—instinct is to keep you safe. Maybe they fear being left out of your life. It could be, too, they feel threatened or diminished by your successes or even envy them. Family feelings can be tangled and complex. That won't change, but you can refuse to let them get in your way.

Your upper limit to comfortable parental, peer or professorial pride is about twenty percent better than they are doing or did. If you go beyond that, the three P's can get uneasy and seemingly ignore what you're doing or even appear to disapprove.

Maybe they'll get over the discomfort, maybe not. The point— since this is Success Therapy, not Family Therapy—is for you to get over it. Don't expect or insist that they be part of the audience. In truth, they may not want to be.

Family, friends, and the home-town crowd occupy important places in your heart and always will, and you love seeing them when you can. What else do you need from them?

DELAYED APPLAUSE

There was very little danger of my success level creating any dissonance between my father Arthur Anderson and myself. He left a legacy in every area of life that anyone would be challenged to live up to. Not only did he give me and my siblings a living model of personal and career success, he made himself an open book by freely discussing his own day-to-day work. Family dinners at our house were family forums for learning.

But Dad is still Dad. It showed when I made what he was absolutely sure was a catastrophically bad career choice right after graduating from college. Other grads would have killed for the job offer I got from a prestigious, internationally recognized company. But I turned it down and pursued a no-salary opportunity with a start-up company 1,200 miles away from where I grew up. In it, I saw the exact opportunity I sought. Here I could make a difference on the ground floor and grow something.

Dad saw something different. To him it looked like I was stepping off a cliff. Despite his reservations, he kept his cool and class. Rather than question my sanity and judgment out loud, he apprised me of job openings for great positions, even set up interviews. After a couple years he stopped. About five years into the venture when it was clear where things were headed, we were driving alone together and he admitted his original reservation about my initial decision and that he would have been wrong to say anything about it. *"You knew yourself better than I did,"* he said. It was a most generous admission which I will never forget.

Dad's recognition and congratulation in that moment meant so much more for both of us than any amount of insincere initial applause. It also illustrates some much-quoted wisdom from the late Bill Gove: **You are responsible <u>to</u> the audience, not <u>for</u> the audience.** I fulfilled my responsibility to my audience member, aka Dad, by doing what I believed was right to the best of my ability and with all my heart. I put on the show based on my own research and my own unique abilities. For a while, my father didn't get it or like it. I knew he thought it was nuts. And it was challenging to NOT take responsibility for his or anybody else's reaction. It's a losing proposition to assume responsibility for things you cannot control, like other people's responses to your show.

Eventually my Dad got it and applauded. Even had he never came around, that would have been alright. I feel like I did right and fulfilled my responsibility to him, the family legacy, and my audience by pursing a dream that would make a difference.

Thank you; you've been a great audience.

SCHOOL RULE

Praise and admiration from the three P's—parents, peers and professors -- is the sweetest reward and the truest measure of success. Work for it. Expect it, because you're entitled to it. If you're not getting it, you should be.

- LESSON FOR LIFE -

Choose your own audience in reality and in your head. You pick the people you most want to please, who get you and want you to realize your potential. Knock yourself out to win their applause. If family and friends give you praise and support, glory in it. If not, it's time to pick a new audience.

14

WHEN YOU'RE FINISHED, YOU CAN GO OUT AND PLAY

ULTIMATE FUN

One of the most brilliant educators I have ever known, now long retired, taught fifth and sixth grades in rural Texas. He turned *"go out and play"* 180 degrees around. His hard-working pupils earned themselves even harder work, using what they learned in class in more challenging brainwork. He sentenced misbehavers and goof-offs to the *"Odd Squad"* where idleness was the rule. Doing nothing turned out to be hard time for do-nothings. They didn't like it.

What did Mr. Great Teacher's kids think was cool and clamor for? Learning more and working harder, of course. Being kids, they still needed to blow off steam like kids, free-form and loud. But the teacher's system, by making hard work its own reward, instilled an important lifelong lesson about productive work and leisure: You need both, and they're both rewarding. Work, however, wins out, and fun goes up with the level of challenge.

For every such genius who makes work a reward we have, sad to say, thousands of teachers, moms and dads, ministers, and workplace managers who reinforce the wrong message. One way or another, they're telling us that work is an onerous burden that you endure for the reward of escaping work.

POP CULTURE IS AGAINST US

It is a challenge, under any circumstance, to unlearn the old, troublesome lessons laid out in this book. But this one is unique in its ubiquity. Is there anyone who doesn't know which day of the week is *"Hump Day"* and why? The expression singles out and celebrates Wednesday for being the workday that finally gets us half-way to end-of-day Friday and the best days of all. Why the best? Because we, or at least a great number of those with conventional employment, don't have to work.

"Hump Day" implies a downhill ride to weekend bliss, after Monday and Tuesday of onerous upward struggle. As if the work week was a one-hill roller coaster, and everybody puts hands up and goes *"Whee!"*

Those who say *"Hump Day"* are ninety-five percent more likely to also say TGIF, maybe before they get out of bed on Friday morning. Anybody not know that means Thank God It's Friday? As mixed initials and the day spelled out—T.G.I. Friday's—it's enshrined on something like 870 restaurants. *"Thank God It's Friday"* was a disco-era movie and same-name sound-track song. A few years after that, disco-haters could rock out to the hit *"Working For The Weekend,"* which you can still bang your head to with Classic Rock radio and old-guy live bands.

The thing lives on, in song, onscreen, in joke-y sayings and workplace chatter. I'm going to stop here, though, because you get it.

PLAY THAT PAYS

Extrapolate from *"When you're finished, you can go out and play,"* and TGIF, and you get things like, *"It's only work if it's not fun,"* or conversely, *"If it's fun, it can't be work."*

These are the credos of the mediocre, the unfulfilled, and the chronically unhappy.

We have never known or even heard of a conspicuously successful person who regarded his or her work as drudgery or worked with the goal of getting away from work. Ultra-successes derive as much if not more fulfillment and pleasure from their on-the-job efforts than from leisure. Sure, they break away now and again to fool around with private vineyards and sail superyachts around their own islands, but such things are designed to recharge the body and spirit and have a purpose all their own.

Leisure and pleasure, in themselves, are never central to a full and happy life. On the other hand, they do have an integral role to play, which I address in an upcoming chapter. It makes clear that off-hours R&R—Reward and Recharge, in my book—are vital, nothing less. This is a related issue, but quite distinct. The subject here is getting maximal enjoyment from work, while you're actually working.

If a barrier stands between fulfillment and work, knock it down! That barrier impedes your own progress. If the job is no fun, there's a good chance that the problem resides in you. Fun, often as not, begins with re-making your mental and work habits. It also begins with permission—which only you can give—to start having fun. On-the-job suffering is very often an option. Quit exercising the option. Lighten up.

But attitude, all by itself, isn't going to do it. Fulfillment on the job means getting serious. Not long-faced serious, but serious the way a good golfer or ball player is serious. Study the game, work on your skills. Deepen your appreciation of the basics, advanced moves, the playing field, equipment, and all the little games within games. The more you know and the more you master, the more fun there is to have.

RESULTS-PRODUCING THOUGHT AND ACTION

YOUR WINNING STRATEGY

Since it's your game, you need your own playbook, training manual, and records.

KNOW THE RULES. Work at all levels is generally governed by rules that are pretty obvious, rules having to do with: start time, duration of play, who's in charge, who's playing various positions and their particular skills and responsibilities, what puts points on the board, draws penalties, or even gets you thrown off the team. Wherever you are, whatever you're doing, there's a system. The wise and successful get with the system.

Amazingly, many others flat-out refuse. Imagine somebody who refuses to learn the rules but insists on playing softball anyway, fighting every inch of the way: *"What do you mean I only get three swings!" "Who says I can't run the bases clockwise?"* Are they loving the game, having fun?

KNOW THE OBJECT. For golfers: the ball in the hole. For sellers: better, bigger-spending buyers, who need and want what you've got. For health care professionals: happy and healthy patients who will continue care and send others to this great practice. There's a point to what you do, which is bigger and better than putting in time and getting paid. Remember the point.

KEEP SCORE AND TRAINING RECORDS. Follow your own career the way sports nuts track players. Memorize all your statistics. Know, day-to-day, whether you're up or down and by how much.

BE YOUR OWN COACH. Show up with a well-rehearsed game plan. When it's over, replay and study your moves. Take advantage of your strengths. Work on your weaknesses. Give yourself the best advice you've got, and see that you follow it.

SURPRISE OTHERS. Satisfactory performance is your starting line, not the finish. Do more than others expect. Always make the second effort.

EXCEED YOURSELF. A little better than you did it last time, every time.

MAKE IT TOUGHER. When you're scoring consistently, raise the basket, tighten the strike zone, move the center-field fence.

ENTHUSE. Psyche up before you show up. Perfect an end-zone dance (or a private, mental equivalent), and do it every time you score. Celebrate small gains, too. Let friends and loved-ones know what's going on so they can cheer for you.

HAVE HEROES. Be inspired by the excellence of others. Watch what they do, how they do it, and emulate them. If you can, do better than them.

GET ON THE TEAM. Your own team. Give the game you're in now at least ninety days of all-out, enthusiastic effort before making any judgements. Quit blaming others, or the job itself, for problems. Take full, 100 percent responsibility for the atmosphere in which you work. Whether or not you like to admit it, you chose what you do for a living. Be open to the idea that the choice was a great one.

You're right. This is a very short chapter. Your lifetime career in your game of choice runs very long. Give it all you've got and have fun!

SCHOOL RULE

Work is work, play is play, and never the twain shall meet. If it's fun, it can't be work, and vice versa.

- LESSON FOR LIFE -

Some of greatest fulfillment, entertainment, and fun can be your work. The better you do it, the harder you go at it, the more it feels like playing, and the more fun you have.

15

WHO'S GOT THE RIGHT ANSWER?

NOBODY HAS IT

"I do! I know the answer!" squeals the Inner Kindergartner, hand jammed up in the air, dying to be called on.

No you don't, the Real World says. Nobody has the right answer, at least not for long. Answers don't count, anyway, not unless they lead to positive, measurable results.

Here we come to a defining difference between pre-adult life and adulthood. For most questions asked in school there's an answer, the correct answer, and Teacher already has it. Success is measured in right answers and getting to them the right ways. Keep doing it and you can qualify for merit scholarships and graduate from college Phi Beta Kappa.

> Unlike school, the world asks questions for which nobody has answers. The future possesses the only answer sheet, and it's forever switching correct and incorrect. This morning's A-plus business decisions may well flunk late in the day. Yesterday's sure-fire failure could make somebody a billionaire next week. You can be entirely right according to all current available knowledge and understanding and go wrong or be all wrong yet succeed brilliantly.

RIGHT / WRONG CRISIS

One of the most wrong things a person can do is to try to be right all the time. It's an equally grave mistake to freeze up and be scared to do anything for fear of being wrong.

While you mull this over, let me share a true-life tale of a serious lapse in judgment that involves a lucky kid making a dumb mistake causing terrible upset and totaling my car. I call the kid lucky not because he walked away from my pancaked car, but because right then, by amazing good fortune, we had with us a famous psychiatrist who was the world expert on right/wrong psychology and how to get straight and stay in control of our lives by controlling how we process actions and outcomes.

Early in my career, we lived on the Texas Hill Country ranch that was home base of our fledgling consultancy and training company. One of the early additions to our family was my fifteen-year-old brother-in-law who needed a more stable home. He was a good kid who settled in with us at the ranch and got a job.

But then one night we got from a call from a neighbor a couple miles down the road who found a teenage boy outside his front door. It took some doing to establish the connection with us, because the poor kid was upset to the point of incoherence. We came on the run and found my brother-in-law and the scene of the precipitating event. Sobbed-out words and the wrecked car told the story: He had come down the steep ranch roadway too fast, couldn't make a tight curve, and rolled the car down the side of the hill.

But the terrible upset wasn't so much about what happened as its meaning and imaginary consequences. Because of his mistake, he thought he was irresponsible and no good, and, he said, *"You guys are going to kick me out. You're not going to let me live here. I won't have anywhere to go!"* He was inconsolable, in a panic. Reassurances from us didn't get through.

Enter the hero of the story, Dr. Maxie C. Maultsby, father of Rational Cognitive Therapy, a friend who happened, right then, to be our guest at the ranch. The next morning Maxie went to work to re-engineer the boy's thinking.

First, the facts: *"You drove too fast, rolled the car, and totaled it. That's what happened."* Then Maxie separated the facts of the accident from the beliefs about the accident: that it meant the boy was irresponsible, that we did not want such a flawed person around and would throw him out, etc. The conversation led to the feelings that resulted from the beliefs. Did the boy like his feelings? Did they get him closer to a desired outcome, or do him any good?

It didn't take long to re-engineer the boy's thinking to something like, *"I've got to go slow and be careful, coming down these steep country roads at night. I've learned a valuable lesson that I never have to learn again. It could save my life..."*

Then came a brilliant Maultsby move: Maxie walked him out to where my unfortunate car lay on its back like a run-over turtle and took a picture of it with the boy standing right next to it. Maxie told him to put the picture where he'd see it every day and remember to live by the day's real lesson:

You choose what you believe about what happens.

WRONG, THE RIGHT WAY

Maxie's healing insight and wisdom were simple, do-able, and effective. If you don't like what you feel right now about what happened, if it's not working for you, the key is to step back and look at your beliefs about what happened and fix them.

Dr. Maultsby taught that problematic right/wrong thinking, one of the enemies of personal and organizational success, dates back millions of years. We're hard-wired to be terrified of making mistakes, because we evolved in 24/7 survival conditions where messing up meant slow death by starvation or quick brutal death by getting killed and possibly eaten. *"Wrong"* equaled *"dead"* or at least too close to it, and on some level, we still believe it.

As Dr. Maultsby observed, nothing in the world is as easy to change as the mind, except the mind itself fights change, because change seems to mean that we were wrong. Still, the doctor had wonderful news for wrong-aphobics:

You don't have to be wrong to change your mind.

On the contrary, changing the mind is often the rightest thing you can do.

Even with no help from deep evolutionary history, the education system would do a wonderful job of reinforcing right/wrong thinking. This chapter started with kindergarten kids crazy to be called on when Teacher says, *"Who's got the right answer?"* That enthusiasm and willingness to speak up and take a shot at answering is pretty much doomed. Eventually the only people who dare to answer are the ones who are absolutely positive they've got it right. And even then, they often sit on their hands.

Out here in the real world your answers come down to decisions to take actions that lead to outcomes, and not too much is straight-up right or wrong, black or white. Most outcomes land in-between, and you won't know where until you make a decision and take a shot. You can't really be sure how it will all come out because things beyond your control go the way they go. Whatever happens, per Dr. Maultsby's common-sense psych, you make the best and most of it in your mind and out in the world.

If things go south—as they usually don't but sometimes do—you can't un-do what's done, but you can control your beliefs, thinking, and resulting feelings. Ask these Dr. Maultsby questions:

- Is this thought true?
- Does this thought get me what I want?
- Does this thought keep me feeling the way I want to feel?

If any or all of the answers are no, re-think the thinking.

Be wrong the right way, and you'll start piling up A-plus outcomes and positive results. Be paralyzed by wrong-aphobia and results will not be forthcoming, because you won't take any action.

Be wrong the right way in your work and communication with others, too. Don't waste a minute, or a nickel's worth of resources, defending an action or position that does not work, just because it's yours. If there's a better route, take it. Don't wait for others to discover a problem you created or worse yet, try to conceal it. Cover Your Behind is a fool's refuge.

Whatever happens, get right with it. And get on with it!

RESULTS-PRODUCING THOUGHT AND ACTION

DEEP RE-THINK

Ask yourself this: What is the biggest mistake you ever made, which you deeply regret?

- Now ask yourself what you believe about what you did and what happened. What does it really mean to you?

- Examine the resulting feelings about yourself and this part of your past.

- Is this how you want to feel?

- Is there anything productive or positive in it for you or anybody else?

Look and think deep to re-examine and re-script your beliefs to get right about what happened. Feel that way, too. It's your choice.

SCHOOL RULE

For every question, every choice, there's one right answer and many wrongs. Your grade in life is the sum of the questions you get right. Choose too many wrong answers and you fail!

- LESSON FOR LIFE -

Be wrong the right way. The most wrong thing you can do is believe that you have to be right all the time. Learn the lessons that can be learned from what you have done in life, right or wrong, good or bad, and then benefit.

16

IT'S NOT FAIR!

THE HAND HE WAS DEALT

So far, I have tried to have a little fun with these dives into recognizing and replacing holdover habits of mind and behavior that cause serious problems for grownups. The fun is often at the expense of overage, oversize schoolkids.

Well, this one's different. The hero of the story is one of the most grown-up grownups I have ever known. It makes me smile to remember him. However, there were moments, many of them, that were nothing to smile about. Life dealt Bob Zampieri a tough hand. Still, he played that hand so beautifully that we who knew and loved him remember him as a winner.

Early in my career I got a call from a Dr. Robert Zampieri who led a thriving dental practice in Fort Lee, New Jersey. He and a group of like-minded dentists wanted me to come east and lead a weekend session on the personal and business aspects of managing and growing their practices. The weekend was a success, and Bob and I began a great working partnership and friendship. Whatever management and communication tools our team provided, he put to good use. All he did in his profession and in his life, he did right.

When I met him, Bob was in his fifties and living a vibrant full life, replete with family, friends, and professional achievement and success. Then, in his sixtieth year, came an agonizing loss to Bob and his family. His son Robbie died in the terrorist attacks on New York City's World Trade Center on September 11, 2001. Bob, his wife Pat, and Robbie's younger brother and sister were devastated.

When tragedy struck, Bob and Pat must have spoken or at least thought the same thing as many thousands of shocked and grieving people who lost loved ones on 9/11: *"It's not fair!"*

But then Bob saw a way to honor his son's memory and help handle his loss by making life more fair for other people's sons and daughters. Opportunity revealed itself in a newspaper article about financial troubles at St. Anthony High School in Jersey City. The scrappy little inner-city private high school was known for fielding the winningest high school basketball program in U.S. History, with 28 state championships and four national titles led by legendary coach Bob Hurley, one of only two high school basketball coaches ever to be inducted into the National Basketball Hall of Fame.

The school and its power basketball team reclaimed and even saved the lives of disadvantaged players, opening doors to college and lifetime opportunities. If the school's doors closed for lack of funding, the doors to better lives would close, too. Bob would not let it happen. He contacted St. Anthony School and set up the Robbie Zampieri Scholarship Fund and for years spearheaded drives to raise money to keep the school alive.

Anyone who knew Bob and Pat was inspired by the good they accomplished in response to the evil that took their son. Redeeming and saving one young life would have been significant, but there were many. And the good lives on in those that have been impacted because of his generosity inspired by something that was not fair.

Cancer finally took Bob's life. The losing fight with disease was not quick or easy, but Dr. Bob Zampieri left the world the way he lived in it—smiling and doing good. He did not cry, *"It's not fair!"* Not on his own behalf...

One of our running themes has been to take control of life. But you can't control everything. You can do right and do good like Bob, and after everything you do there remains randomness. Living life can be a lot like playing poker. You can't control the cards you're dealt. It's your hand, and nobody else's.

WHAT YOU CAN CONTROL IS HOW YOU PLAY IT.

Nowhere is it written that life is fair. The Bible and every other source of mature thought and spiritual wisdom tells us, very explicitly, that it is not. All sorts of evidence—innocent people victimized by disasters, bad people who enjoy fabulous wealth and live to ripe old ages—says the same thing. Much of what happens in this world is incredibly cruel and unjust, and it isn't in our power to make it kind and just. A significant part of getting out of grade school and growing up is learning to accept, as Shakespeare's Hamlet put it, *"the slings and arrows of outrageous fortune."* Life's inequities and undeserved, out-of-the-blue setbacks and catastrophes must be accepted if we are to get on with living. Accept them even when they mean the end of life.

Like Dr. Bob Zampieri.

Getting straight with the notion of fairness and what we can rightfully expect in life is one of the toughest lessons for grownups to learn and take to heart. On the flip side, the old kindergarten howl of protest, *"It's not fair!"* is especially tough to get out of one's head. Tough either way because, well, stuff happens that's tough to understand and deal with. It's tougher still because we were brought up to expect and even demand fair play and fair treatment. But reality does not play fair, at least not the way fairness was first defined for us.

As ever, the seeds of trouble aren't trouble at all in childhood. Parents and teachers have a moral obligation to teach children to deal honestly and equitably with others, to respect others' dignity, property and privacy, to expect, even insist, that the group and its authority figures not show favoritism toward some, or prejudice against others—to be, in a word, fair.

Though right for nurturing and training our young, enforced fairness and wraparound security is a poor model for the grownup world. There are seeds here that lead to passivity, learned helplessness, and feelings of entitlement that get in the way of achievement.

Narcissistic entitlement, which says the world owes us whatever we want whether we earned it or not, is a problem of near-crisis proportions. Funny thing about a sense of entitlement—it can effectively prevent you from getting whatever you feel entitled to! The more you tell yourself, *"It's not fair!"* the more you won't get what you think is fair.

So far, we have addressed violated expectations, which are pretty much guaranteed in growing up. People old enough to know better howl, *"It's not fair!"* just because reality doesn't dote on them and take care of them like Mom and Dad and Teacher did.

Entitled individuals can be catastrophically unprepared to accept and deal with real reversals that arrive sooner or later, no matter what. There's danger that *"It's not fair!"* can lead to a paralyzing condition called Stuck In Suffering. Victims fixate on the gap between What Is in the real world and What Ought To Be in some ideal world in their heads. There's hope and opportunity all around, there for the taking, but they don't take it because all they can see and feel is what the world didn't give them.

RESULTS-PRODUCING THOUGHT AND ACTION

LISTEN AND LOOK WITHIN

This one's quick on paper and challenging in practical application. It's all about getting straight with yourself and straight with the realities of life where happenstance has a role.

Go quiet and listen to inner voices. If you pick up on Little You yelling, *"It's not fair!"* and feeling aggrieved, look deeper. Most of the time, this isn't about fairness at all, and the real meaning is more like, *"Nobody told me it would be like this!"* or *"This is tougher than I thought it would be!"* If you are honest with yourself, you'll recognize the complaint as a disguised admission of *"I don't like it!"* or even *"I knew it could happen, but I didn't think it could happen to me!"* You're hearing the voice of the Inner Kindergartner bawling for somebody big to come to the rescue. The next time your Inner Kindergartner starts crying, *"It's not fair!"* take a good look at yourself and your circumstances. Could be that things are much more fair than you'd like to admit. Could be that you're just crying for a break that nobody else gets, either.

Note: When you suffer truly serious loss and misfortune, an initial reaction of *"It's not fair!"* is completely understandable. Still, it ultimately gets you nowhere. Grieving, acceptance, and working-through take time, sure, but the ultimate goal is always to recover and carry on. Whatever life deals out, you must pick up your cards and play your hand.

SCHOOL RULE

Fairness as it was defined for us is something to be counted on. Yesteryear's expectations are good forever. If the world doesn't treat you fairly by those terms, sit down and howl, and somebody Big will make it right.

- LESSON FOR LIFE -

The world couldn't care less about what you expect, what you're used to, what you're sure you deserve, and what we were taught to call Fair. When there's change, when the hand is dealt, adapting to it is the name of the game. So go ahead, play the hand you're dealt, and play it well.

Nearly Everything I Learned In Kindergarten Screwed Me Up!

17

It's Milk and Cookie Time

COOKIE CONSPIRACY

Oops, I've just revealed my age. But Milk and Cookie Time is still in my head, as it is for many of us who grew up before widespread nut allergies, lactose and gluten intolerance, and the like.

For most of us kids, back in the day, a cookie was never just a cookie. It was coin of the realm, exchangeable for happiness. If Mom or Grammy gave you a cookie you had a token of love, also a good-conduct medal because bad kids don't get cookies. A cookie could be a license to make noise and run around with your friends. At the end of dinner it meant you survived the liver and lima beans, and in a couple minutes you could clear the table and get the heck away from the grownups.

Kindergarten did its part at Milk and Cookie Time. Here the cookie and itty-bitty carton of moo juice signaled a particularly relaxed and sociable period that was always greeted with cheers and oh-boys from the class and a big smile from Teacher.

Whoever started school lukewarm about cookies would surely be converted by June. What if little Genevieve liked artichoke hearts or olives better? Bringing her own was probably against the rules, and if she could do it, she'd have to listen to all the other kids going *"Ewwww."* In an atmosphere of institutionalized and conventionalized pleasure, there's no real line between group indulgence and self-indulgence. And there's very little room for originality.

Please, don't get the wrong idea about me and cookies. Now and again I enjoy one myself, and I have no problem treating kids with cookies and other sweets, in healthy moderation of course. Still, though, there's a disturbing element in this whole cookie business. It's a primary model for something we grownups need to recognize and overcome. If we don't, our precious—make that priceless—opportunities to relax, recharge, re-center, and find joy will be on somebody else's terms.

Though bigger now, with pricier cookies, the other kids still hoot and holler about Milk and Cookie Time, doing everything they can to get us to buy into their particular brands of fun. And we do buy in. We give others power over things that ought to be ours and ours alone—our pleasures. Nobody should be telling us what's entertaining, what's relaxing, what's beautiful, what's delicious. But somebody does tell us day and night.

LIBERATING LEISURE

Billions upon billions of dollars go into mass-producing treats and toys for grownups. Billions more are spent to convince us that the stuff is worth the money and/or debt load because it's a dream come true. Look at online and magazine ads, commercials, billboards—nothing but cookies! Some are bubbly and come in bottles, $75 a pop. Some set you back $90,000, burn premium fuel only, go 150 miles an hour. Some cookies are shaped like vacation, tennis at Hilton Head, bassin' in Bull Shoals Lake, or shaking Mickey and Minnie's paws at the gates of the Magic Kingdom.

Beware of all this Buy Me/Be Happy! For one thing, impulsive nonessential purchases are enemies of fiscal discipline and personal savings. They're also Visa and Mastercard's best friend. But we'll skip over the financial hazards and focus on personal sovereignty. That, and nothing less, is at stake.

Success in leisure takes every bit as much discipline as success at work. To truly reward yourself for your efforts and hard-earned achievements, you must tune out the hard selling and peer pressure and decide exactly what suits you.

Take a good look at how you fill time away from the job, how you're spending the money that's left over after the basic needs have been met.

People who count, count. They count where the minutes and dollars are going. They absolutely do not let other people tell them where and how their precious, irreplaceable personal time and resources ought to be spent.

R&R—REWARD AND RECHARGE

Whether great big rewards for major achievements or daily quick recharges, treating yourself should serve two main functions. For one, it's your own personal incentive program. You give yourself something to look forward to for a job well-done or goal accomplished, proportional to what's achieved.

One unique payoff for reaching a professional milestone comes to mind: My late business partner Walter B. Hailey, who made his first fortune in insurance sales, once decided to treat himself to a pedicure on the beach in Bermuda when he brought in a million dollars in new business.

Walter kept up his million-dollar/Bermuda ritual for a while. Why that, on that particular island? Who knows? One person's gift to triumphal self is another's, *"What the heck?"* You might as well ask why I have a Harley Davidson Screaming Eagle Convertible CVO motorcycle out in the garage. The monster soft tail holds a place of honor because, in part, of what it represents in terms of reward for accomplishment.

On an almost daily basis, my Harley also serves the Second R function, just as vital as the first. Recharging.

The bike takes me to places where I need to go. As soon as I'm out on the road, I'm there. Even locales I see on a near-daily basis become magic destinations and jump-offs to wondrous side roads I never drive in my truck. I like the truck well enough as reliable, efficient, utilitarian transportation. But when I drive it, I'm caged up and not out in the world, smelling the smells, feeling the wind and weather, with nothing between me and the glories of the day that I am always part of on my motorcycle.

Water works wonders for me, too, to the point that there's a standing joke around here about my *"board meetings,"* which are meets with my wakeboard or surfboard behind the boat on the lake that's two minutes from my house.

An hour on the lake can work the same restorative magic as one-hour roadies on the Harley. I come back to a place different than what I left, energized and with a clear head. Riding and wakeboarding might not do the same for you, but something surely will, and you owe it to yourself to discover it and reward yourself with short-term breaks. You'll know you've got it right when you come back invigorated and in a more upbeat and creative state of mind. You'll benefit before breaks, too, because it's motivating to have something near-term to look forward to.

Nothing in the world is quite so just-right, so perfect, as giving yourself the gifts, small and large, that really are gifts, enhancing your life the way you want to live it. To go back to the way we started this chapter—with cookies—grownup leisure is Milk and Cookie Time your way, with original-recipe cookies served whenever and however you want them.

Take care that the treats you pick are assets, not liabilities. Assets pay back more than they cost. Their value to you increases over time—not necessarily in dollars, but in some way that is real to you. They get you closer to your goals and add to the existence of you and those you care about. If you don't come back in a better state—like, say, if you get drunk and stay up to all hours and come to work hung over—your reward is actually punishment in disguise. Liabilities might feel wonderful momentarily, but they take more than they give. Very often you're still paying after they've totally lost their worth.

It's hazardous not to build R&R into your life. If you don't, you may be setting yourself up for A&E—Addiction and Escape. Every action in life is either goal-achieving or tension-relieving. The tension relievers, good only right now, are what get us into trouble. Your own chosen milk and cookie time can either be goal achieving R&R or tension relieving A&E. Choose carefully.

RESULTS PRODUCING THOUGHT AND ACTION

A. Spend an hour or as many minutes as you can spare alone in a peaceful spot.

B. Let your mind go quiet, then picture and feel the things that please you most, that are perfect for you, such as the company of certain people, movies, shows, making or just enjoying music, art, hobbies, athletics, foods, favorite places. There are no rules here except your own personal delight and life enhancement. Some may be free, some expensive, some in the backyard and others 8,000 miles away.

C. Ask and answer: Are you doing enough of the things that really feed you and bring joy?

D. At least a few of your perfect things are going to be cheap if not free, quick, and close to home. Make a plan to gift yourself with one of these refreshers as soon as you possibly can. Make another plan to incorporate at least one moment of joy and personal renewal—perfect just for you—every single day.

E. When you've got the daily R&R habit, make a Grand Plan. Daydream your way to a supreme personal reward and a crowning achievement that will earn it. Start accomplishing now. And, when you've earned it, celebrate and glory in your gift to yourself!

SCHOOL RULE

Fun is what everybody, large and small, says is fun. To know what you want, watch what others are yelling about and clamoring for.

- LESSON FOR LIFE -

Reward and Recharge are absolutely necessary and absolutely personal. And nobody but you can tell you what your cookies are.

18

Who Wants to Clean the Board?

WE ALL DO, TEACHER

We really do. Long before we knew what *"clean slate"* meant figuratively, we knew what it meant literally, and we loved it. Back in the day kids vied for the privilege of cleaning the great big chalkboard at the front of the room. I remember, fresh as yesterday, dying to be one of the chosen when Teacher asked for volunteers.

Toward class dismissal on Friday kids were eager to perform that very special job. After the usual go-over with dry felt erasers, the privileged made another more meticulous pass with damp cloths. Each swipe wiped away dust and messy bits of words and numbers and left behind pristine blankness.

That Friday blackboard was as beautiful as a still pond in the wilderness. It looked like renewal, a fresh start, a spotless and perfect break from the cluttered and chaotic past. Even so close to the beginnings of our own lives, we longed for such things.

And we still do more than ever.

Yes, we all want to clean the board, the one on the inside, where all our limiting beliefs, bad habits, self-doubts and self-sabotaging messages are written. We'd like to wipe away the painful and messy parts of our personal histories and start again with our heads, spirits, and our whole lives like that freshly-cleaned, shiny board.

GHOST WRITING

Let's go back and sneak into the classroom after school. We'll turn on the lights and study the board a little more closely to see what's really there instead of what we want to see.

As the board dries from the damp cleaning, it loses its sheen, showing a patch or two of unwiped dust and cryptic bits of letters and numbers. The boards back in my school always bore a scribble or two that refused to go away. Come Monday morning, we'd contemplate that ghost writing, which was not good to look upon.

It didn't trouble us for long, though, because Teacher made it go away. How? With special spray, an electric eraser? No, by starting a new lesson, scratching and banging out new stuff on the board in a cloud of chalk dust. The ghost writing still showed if you looked close, but nobody looked or cared.

There are powerful life lessons in the chalkboard about cognitive, emotional, and spiritual cleansing and renewal and how to effect lasting life changes.

Now and again we must make the effort to clean our own boards, to wipe away the past for greater clarity in the present. But if all we do is erase, the past starts re-appearing like the ghost writing on the board.

In truth, if a chalkboard operated like the human psyche, just sitting and looking would bring back whole sentences and numbers and drawings. Everything ever put on the board would reappear. Biggest and boldest, in lurid neon colors, would be the stuff we never want to see again.

CHUNK THE JUNK

Our seminars begin with a ritual erasure of the past. **Chunk The Junk**, we call it, *"Chunk"* for *"throw"* or, as in this case, *"throw away."*

Participants each write down a troublesome personal issue. Guilty secrets, old anger, unspoken hurt, old habits, hurt, fear, jealousy, betrayal—all sorts of ugliness bubbles up, but we don't ask people to share their junk. They just have to write it down on paper that they crumple and throw into a big trash can.

You can feel the room get lighter and brighter. In the emotional dimension, that receptacle holds tons of toxic waste. One drop could make everybody miserable.

What comes next? Do we go *"Ahhh"* and sit in the sunshine and share thoughts about inner cleansing and renewal? No way! We charge hard into the next session with practical, do-able new material all day, then next morning get up with the sun and get back at it.

Junk Chunking is a start; that's all. With no new engagement and challenge, the bad stuff comes back.

RESULTS-PRODUCING ACTION AND THOUGHT

For this one you'll need a pad of lined writing paper, something like a legal pad or spiral-bound stenographer's notebook. Partially used-up is fine, because ten pages or so suffice. The computer won't do it on this one, by-the-way. There is emotional and psychological power in having to write it down on paper, the old-fashioned way.

PART ONE
Rip out the first clean page and **Chunk Your Junk**.

Likely you already have an item in mind. It's unfixable, ugly, and in the way. You bang into it and cause yourself pain but nevertheless keep it in heart and/or mind. Well, that ends here. Write a few words for the junk on your sheet of paper. Things like *"Hating on Andy," "Chardonnay," "Mom loved Jean more," "Shirley's husband," "Secret smoking,"* and *"Binge eating"* will do, because you know the details and essence of the problem you need to lose.

Crumple up the paper and chunk it. It was junk but now it is absolutely nothing, because it's gone.

CAUTION: Great as it feels, don't dwell on what just happened. Donated toasters and shoes don't come back from Goodwill when you think about them, but inner junk surely does. You can't force it out of mind by refusing to think about it, either, because you can't not-think about anything. I'll prove it: Don't think about the Statue of Liberty. Now don't think about that old nonsense with Andy. What did you just think?

Chunk more junk when you feel the need.

PART TWO

Immediately post-junk-chunk, you should plunge into new thought and action.

On top of the first clean sheet in your pad, write this big and bold: **ACTION IDEAS TO IMPROVE MY RESULTS**.

For young participants at Eagle U, we make it **20 Action Ideas** and get them going on a numbered list to fill in throughout their week. All the while, they're getting gimmies for their lists because the takeaways in all our sessions involve specific actions—things to do that bring positive outcomes in school, extracurriculars, career, and all areas of life. By week's end, the 20 Action Ideas explode to fifty or more.

Build your own list with care and serious purpose. This is not a wish list or goals to aspire to. It is serious action to undertake now or as soon as practically possible. What you put on the list, you mean to do—unless, of course, you're already doing it.

Feel free to use this book as an Action Idea starter kit. Flip back through your pages for things like:

- Write down my goals, review them every day, keep them where I can see them. (Chapter 11: Can I Go To The Bathroom?)

- Get a Mentor without actually using the M-word and scaring him/her away. (Chapter 6: My Name Is Miss Jones)

- Copy Genius. (Chapter 3: Do Your Own Work)

- Sync up with your organization's leadership. (Chapter 10: Teacher's Pet!)

- Ask good questions and get good answers every day. (Chapter 7: Any Questions?)

You can pick up more than twenty for the list right in these pages, because this book was conceived and written in keeping with what I deeply believe is the true Philosophy of Education: **The only purpose of education is not knowledge; it's results-producing action.**

VALEDICTORY

As has been written here, over and over, no one is throwing shade on formal education and educators, i.e. school and Teacher. You need knowledge taught in class. You need more from school than that, actually, to get the hang of interacting with others like a civilized human being. School, starting in Kindergarten, was about **learning**. But productive and successful grownup life is about **being** and **doing**. Life rules aren't school rules. And school smarts aren't smart enough.

Remember, the school we keep going back to isn't really John Paul Jones Elementary, St. Holiness Grade School or wherever you attended K through 6. It's the schoolhouse between the ears where many grownups try to hide from the here-and-now by being a good little gold-star kid.

The desire for a certain superficial kind of perfection—like the old damp-cleaned Friday chalkboard—is a childish desire, and a danger to anyone but children. With so much to be done, and so little time for doing it, there just isn't time for pseudo-perfection, which contributes nothing to the final result.

If you wait for the world to look like Teacher's just-cleaned blackboard, you're waiting for a perfect start.

You'll wait forever.

You can't start from perfection, but you can start your journey toward perfection from exactly where you are—this messy and imperfect here and now.

If there's a voice telling you to wait for something—until the weekend's over, you get back from vacation, finish the department's annual report, sell the condo, pay off the VISA card, get on a workout schedule and lose 15 pounds—before you start doing what you should be doing this instant, you're listening to the Inner Kindergartner.

It's time to quit listening. Do it before you get to the bottom of this page, before the second hand gets to the twelve, before another beat of the heart. Its beats are numbered, as are your days.

Do with your inner kid what your grownups once did with you. Take the kid through the schoolhouse door and down the hall to Room 1. Watch all the sweet little people settle into their chairs. Be comforting if there's fear. Drop a tear, if you're feeling sentimental. Tell Teacher how much you admire the profession.

Then run back into the Grownup World and stay there!

For you, and me, now and forever...

SCHOOL'S OUT!

NO MORE SCHOOL RULES — You know what they are, and why you need new ones.

NO MORE LESSONS — You know what you need to learn.

NO MORE ASSIGNMENTS — You know what you need to do.

NO MORE BOOK — Time to write your own, in life.

SCHOOL'S OUT!!!

OTHER BOOKS BY THE AUTHOR
The Yes Press / Crown Council

These are just a few of the favorite things we have created over the years that people rave about. Order below and enjoy!

All the books are available at **http://shop.crowncouncil.com**

 **The 13 Biggest Mistakes Parents Make and How to Avoid Them**

 **The Culture of Success**

You Can Do It Better

You Can Do It Too

You Can Do It Best

You Can Do It 365 Days Better

Born From Fire

Never Stand Alone

See Deeper

ABOUT THE AUTHOR

Steven J. Anderson is an entrepreneur, author, presenter, philanthropist, and agent for creating a Culture of Success.

You can find him at www.StevenJAnderson.com

Every culture is a cumulation of the people in it. *Nearly Everything I Learned in Kindergarten Screwed Me Up!* is the guide for taking personal responsibility for creating a Culture of Success no matter your position in the organization.

As an entrepreneur, Steve has co-created multiple organizational cultures. Here are just a few examples of many:

The Crown Council - www.CrownCouncil.com - Creating a Culture of Success in Your Practice. The home for top dental practices that are committed to an ongoing, never-ending process of improving and delivering exceptional clinical care and patient service in a Culture of Success. For information call: 1-800-CROWN-58 or log onto www.CrownCouncil.info

Total Patient Service Institute - www.TotalPatientSerice.com - Team specific training, live seminars, and in-office coaching for creating a Culture of Success.

Smiles for Life Foundation – Dentistry's leading cause-related campaign having raised nearly $50 million for children's charitable causes world-wide. Discover how you can participate as a patient or a practice by logging onto www. SmilesForLife.org.

Eagle University – www.EagleUniversity.org - Youth leadership training helping high school and college age students get a 7 year head start on their career. Week long Eagle U courses give students the secrets, skills, and strategies to advance their careers and their lives beyond the ordinary.

As a presenter, Steve speaks at conventions and meetings around the world.

For more information on having a presentation at your next meeting, log onto www.StevenJAnderson.com or call: 1-877-399-8677